# THE WONDER OF

# AMERICAN TOYS

## 1920-1950

by Charles Dee Sharp

COLLECTORS PRESS

*For a free catalog contact:*
Collectors Press, Inc.
P.O. Box 230986
Portland, Oregon 97281
Toll-free 1-800-423-1848
www.collectorspress.com

*Design:* Overland Agency, Inc.
*Editing:* Ann Granning Bennett
*Photography:* Larry Evans, Charles Dee Sharp, Robert Frerck

Printed in Singapore
First American Edition
9 8 7 6 5 4 3 2 1

Library of Congress Cataloging-in-Publication Data

Sharp, Charles Dee.
    The wonder of American toys, 1920-1950 / by Charles Dee Sharp.
        p. cm.
    Includes bibliographical references.
    ISBN 1-888054-70-0 (alk. paper)
    1. Toys—Collectors and collecting—United States—Catalogs.
  2. Toys—United States—History.  I. Title.
NK9509.65.U6 S53 2002
688.7'2'0973075—dc21

*"How can you — why would you —
analyze a passion?"*
                                    – overheard conversation


for my treasured grandchildren,
Jessica and Jacob

# THE WONDER OF

# AMERICAN

# TOYS

## 1920-1950

### by Charles Dee Sharp

COLLECTORS PRESS

Portland, Oregon

# contents

# rarity guide

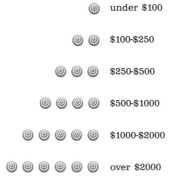

◎    under $100

◎ ◎    $100-$250

◎ ◎ ◎    $250-$500

◎ ◎ ◎ ◎    $500-$1000

◎ ◎ ◎ ◎ ◎    $1000-$2000

◎ ◎ ◎ ◎ ◎ ◎    over $2000

Please note: The value of a toy is subjective. Primary determinants are rarity, desirability (not age), and condition. Also the region in which it appears plays a factor in its value, but this is less so since the advent of the Internet.

# foreword

Never before and never again, we may suppose, will there be such a wide and wondrous array of toys as appeared in America after the First World War and until shortly after the Second World War. This book is a celebration of the culture that formed them, the designers and manufacturers who produced them and, most especially, the toys themselves.

Most of the toys portrayed in this book are ones that I collected over an eighteen-year period. Except for fifty or sixty toys that I could not bear to part with, they are gone now, sold at auction, released back out into the world to continue their salutary affects: at a time when I was chronically incapacitated, these toys were instrumental in helping me get back my spirit and my legs — of enabling me, instead of sinking deep into a wheelchair, of enjoying, once again, a level playing field in life's ongoing pursuit of happiness. Before bidding them goodbye, however, photographs were made of them, a kind of personal memorialization. Given the reflection of their era that they mirrored and the love, and the JOY, that they engendered both then and still today, it's not probable, I think, that the world will ever see their like again.

# acknowledgments

The following are some of the people who, knowingly and unknowingly, were instrumental in the creation of this book —

Judith Sharp (my wife)

Russell and Osie Sharp
(my parents)

Dudley Maddox (my sidekick)

Roger McDougal

Gerrit Beverwyck

Dick Martin

Dr. John Garvin

Joe McGarry

Jim Newark

Gregg Loesser

Hy Roth

Bill Eubank

Bob Frerck

Dr. Bill and Mary Furnish

Wayne Banchik

Dale Kelly

Sonny Hatfield

Chuck Maranto

Don E. Sharp

Nabile and Assad Baaklini

Diane L. Cosentino

*My deepest thanks.*

CDS

# introduction

The golden age of any culture or endeavor is rarely recognized as such during its time. Those of us who grew up in what today is thought of as the Golden Age of American toys — from about 1920 until the early 1950s — assumed that the toys proliferating in the Woolworth and Kresge five-and-dime stores, the department stores, the Wards, Sears, Spiegel, and F.A.O. Schwartz catalogs, would always be there; that they would exist forever in the present; that history, as regards these toys, had stopped.

We've since realized how wrong we were.

Unlike toys manufactured in Europe in earlier years, the hundreds of American toys produced during this period, the so-called Late Industrial Age, were made for the proletariat, the hoi-polloi. They were mass-produced to be sold by the millions, the vast majority for less than a dollar – for fifty cents, a quarter, many for a dime.* Today, a great many of these toys sell for hundreds and even thousands of dollars, not entirely because of their relative scarcity (junked in war-time metal scrap drives, worn out from use, or simply "outgrown"), but because we live in a vastly different era, an era in which the appeal of these toys, their aesthetic charm, craftsmanship, and ingeniousness, is achingly apparent. They have become objects of connoisseurship. With their simplicity, integrity, and incredible vitality, they have an aura; there is something about these toys. They are like pieces of sculpture, timeless, yet fixed in time. Produced between the twentieth century's two World Wars and shortly afterwards, these toys, besides being playthings for children, are reflections of a nation defining itself, an Art Moderne time when women's hemlines were rising and women were allowed to vote; when national radio networks allowed people across the country to hear the same news, music, and entertainment; when men wore fedoras and women wore gloves and when a weekly trip to the movies was habitual and drugs and out-of-wedlock births were few. From the construction of the Panama Canal (Wolverine's "Panama" Pile Driver), the Model-T car (Marx's Amos 'n' Andy taxi), the Depression (Nifty's Hi-Way Henry), World War II (hundreds of exam-

*"Whether one has little to say or writes a book about toys (there is evidence, after all, that our caveman ancestors' children, forty-thousand years ago, made games of stones), it all comes to the same thing: toys are a primordial necessity, like eating. They have always been and will always be. What else does one need to know?"*

– DICK MARTIN, ARTIST/COLLECTOR

ples), to a view of the future in which everything seemed possible (Marx's plastic Robert the Robot) — it was all mirrored in America's toys.

The toys in this book defined material virtues that our society thought worthy of honor. Offering various forms of escape and promises of mastery, these toys often captured the essence of those things better than the things themselves. Toys, more often than not, have a way of doing this as nothing else can — not by modeling, or miniaturizing the object to be delicately admired, but by transposing the object's size, shape, color, and action into a feasible approximation that can be held in your hand as you would a gem or an heirloom — and played with. (A need, we are told, not only of humans but of most living creatures.) Material objects such as toys tell us things that people can't — not least how they feel in your hand (as they must have, you conjecture in a kind of wonder, in previous hands).

Toys initially affect us through our central nervous system, only later through our intellect. Something happens when we play with, or even simply look at, an admired toy: the toy becomes a "we," not an "it" (magic occurs). Relaxing with his toys, the adult collector engages serenity. Looking at them, rearranging them on their shelves, dusting them — through these actions, they become a kind of inanimate life force. Even when fatigued or ill (especially then), the collector resonates with the wonder of how fantastic it is that mankind can have built ships and trains, automobiles and airplanes, circuses and games, and that here, on the collector's shelves, are those achievements, representations that invite themselves to be held in your hand and interacted with. Is that not entrancing? Healthful and fulfilling? Really wonderful?

It's astonishing. We've all seen the phenomenon again and again: what happens to a man or woman's countenance when he or she has their picture taken with a recently acquired toy, doll, or game from their childhood — the radiant, guileless smile that's slathered across their suddenly ageless face. Presumably it's because they've transported themselves back to an earlier time when the world's possibilities lay before them, when all was wonder and heaven's gate opened wide.

There's something else too: old toys are full of love. Early last century, a child loved the toy that we now possess, a child who played with it for untold hours and seasons. Despite its dents or paint chips or rust or missing parts, the love imparted to it has not leached away. It's sublimated, but the love is still there. We know it because we can intuit it. We know it because we know it. There is **something** about these old toys.

An inner necessity drives the collector of toys — for reasons of aesthetics, of history, even of anthropology. But mainly collecting seems to begin because of the toys we had, or didn't have, in childhood — dormant memories carried into adulthood that are one day triggered into consciousness and a certain toy (a rich mythology), is remembered. And we start to brood: Does the toy still exist? Might I find it?

Thus does The Hunt begin. And as the collector roams far and wide, seeking his bliss in the most unlikely places, the hopeful, goading thought plays in his psyche like a mantra: **You never know**.

Often, after finding — or not finding — the coveted toy, interest in others of its kind is aroused, each acquisition filling an interior chasm not previously known to exist. It may not be the toy itself that's identified with so much as it is what the toy expresses. Thus does involvement with a given toy or toys become a kind of research into one's personhood, into the temporal/existential questions and attitudes one holds within. A private affair, call it.

Collecting as an avocation or hobby is several things at once: a way of making connections to one's past, of enhancing one's environment, of expressing who one is. A way, finally, of going beyond one's mundane self. In today's cultural reckoning, no less than today's political and military reckoning, collecting old toys animates us to reflect deeply about who we were and are.

Rarely are any two collections the same. The depth of one's pocketbook aside, everyone makes his or her own rules. For some collectors, there are no rules, everything being opportunistic and depending on the mood one finds oneself in when confronted by the possibility of acquisi-
tion. Most collections are more than the sum of their parts. They tell an interior story as well as an exterior story — often stories within stories. It's with both hope and forbearing that the collector says to his or her family and friends, "I don't say these things I've collected are important to you or to the world, but they're important to me. I think they're wonderful. Don't you agree? Don't you? Really? Don't you? (It's entirely possible, of course, that they may not.)

After handling toys for a while (and becoming used to their improbably high and ever-rising prices), you begin to recognize the manufacturer of a given toy by its look. You may also begin to wonder why, of two similar toys, one was more popular when first sold than the other, and remains so today. What is there about a typical Chein toy, for instance, that is "better" than a typical Courtland toy, an early Fisher-Price than a Gong-Bell? Was Louis Marx the "King of Toys" (as the December 11, 1955, cover story in Time magazine proclaimed) because he was a great businessman, had a greater sales force (it was small), or was it, more than any other consideration, because he hired superior artists/designers? Was not the most crucial element of all, even more than its function or cost, the toy's visual appeal to child and parent alike?

There is something about the toys in this book, something that was, and remains, peculiarly American — grace notes, if you will, of what existed in America's historic landscape.* Affirmations of life, they are

*Not every toy illustrated in this book can be considered a "grace note." Some of them were casually, if not viciously, racist.

retrievers of our sense of wonder, urging us away from an ever insistent Now toward an affective sense of the past (memory being the thing that gives us our identity). They speak to the universal.

There is **something** about these old toys.

Early Freudian theorists related collecting to attitudes toward toilet training; to the hunt of prey; to sexual desire. Later psychoanalytic thought linked collecting to self-worth; to gaining mastery over something; a salve for emotional pain experienced in childhood (think of Citizen Kane, of Kane's lost childhood sled, "Rosebud"). Other reasons were formulated: pride of possession ("It's mine!"); a sense of fixity; a sense of completion; a Proustian retrieval of lost bliss. (It is said that nostalgia — a mix of memory and desire — may be the most beautiful word in any language. Not you, of course, and not me, but for some collectors — more never being enough — it can also be the most dangerous.) There is also, alas, the unknowable sanctum sanctorum collector who, owner of an especially rare acquisition, holds it for himself alone, seldom allows it to be seen by others and disallows any photograph of it.

There are obvious other reasons for collecting: the preservation of history; financial investment; a bulwark against the coming of our inevitable night. Let it also be noted that there are those who insist that they collect for the simple reason that they take pleasure in certain objects and "For no other reason! None! That's it!"

"BEAUTY: that which delights the senses or exalts the mind; a particularly good example of a specimen or thing." German philosopher Immanuel Kant believed that the concept of beauty was a universal one, beyond the reach of time, fashion, or individual whim. We may not say, he said, that everyone must agree with our proclamation, but that beauty inspires a feeling that everyone should agree; that beauty, the judgment of it, carries an assertion of authority, of universality.

Contemporary judgment, on the other hand, declaims that beauty cannot aver universality but is a product of experience, usefulness, and culturally based value judgments made in response to contemporary social-political-economic needs.

Such arguments, of course, are for academics, not toy collectors who know that the toy they've just acquired, or still hunt for, was first provided to a child as an expression of love and caring, that that toy and others like it are the touchstones of imagination, that such toys trigger visions of things that once were, that are, that can never be, that just might be. Toy collectors understand that toys have a context, that they tell a story. That toys are epiphanous and that they are lenses through which to examine and illuminate a cultural/historical era — what was going on in the zeitgeist. And that they remind us how little the amusements of grownups differ from those of their children. That toys are not just for children.

"A toy collector at a toy show," reminisced

a collector," — it's like playing tag when you were a kid. I mean you're always smiling when you play tag — you go outside yourself, you're just smiling, smiling, smiling."

I last played tag more than a half century ago. But hearing this remark, I knew immediately that playing tag was the perfect analogy to collecting toys: At a toy show, or wherever else you may find them, you're able to get Home without being Tagged Out.

And so, in this very different, daunting, and darker mood of today, it's with a very real sense of privilege and immeasurable pleasure that I have the opportunity to present herein some of toys we used to have, once upon a time in America.

CDS

"The toy is the child's first introduction to art."

– CHARLES BEAUDELAIRE

# down on the farm

"Toys, like great art, have the power to transform. They build a bridge between worlds."

– ARNOLD MOORE

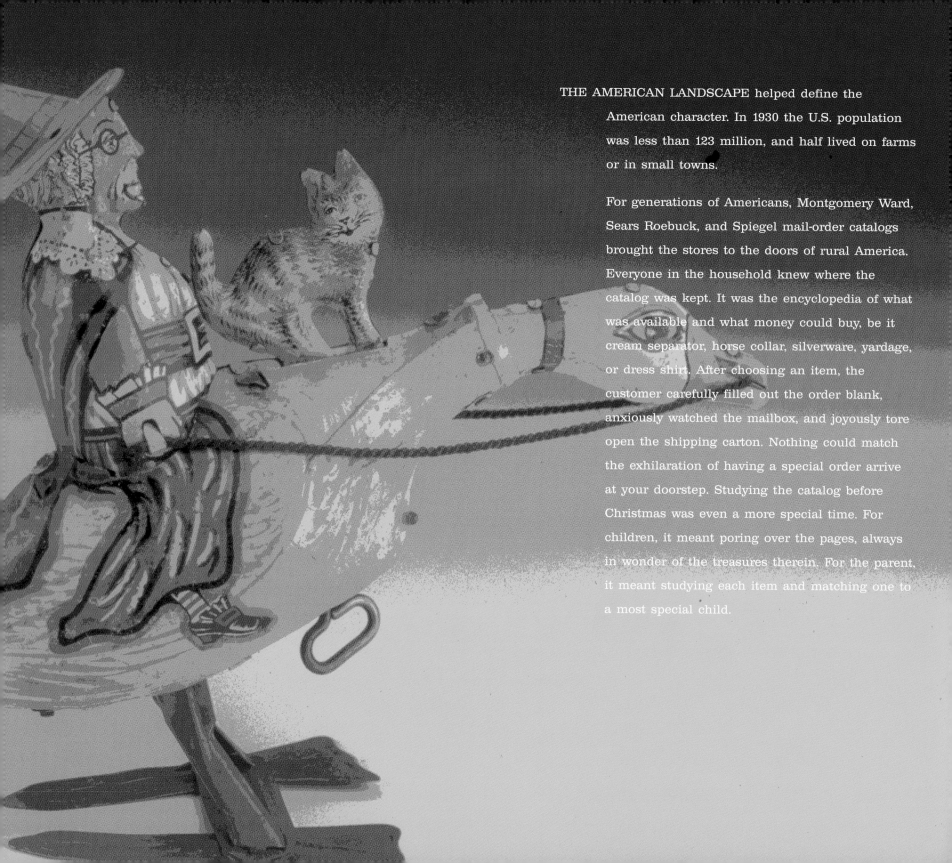

THE AMERICAN LANDSCAPE helped define the American character. In 1930 the U.S. population was less than 123 million, and half lived on farms or in small towns.

For generations of Americans, Montgomery Ward, Sears Roebuck, and Spiegel mail-order catalogs brought the stores to the doors of rural America. Everyone in the household knew where the catalog was kept. It was the encyclopedia of what was available and what money could buy, be it cream separator, horse collar, silverware, yardage, or dress shirt. After choosing an item, the customer carefully filled out the order blank, anxiously watched the mailbox, and joyously tore open the shipping carton. Nothing could match the exhilaration of having a special order arrive at your doorstep. Studying the catalog before Christmas was even a more special time. For children, it meant poring over the pages, always in wonder of the treasures therein. For the parent, it meant studying each item and matching one to a most special child.

PUREBRED STOCK FARM   48 PIECES   MANUFACTURER UNKNOWN   1934   $1.19

"The animals are the champions you see in the Stock shows — authentic types, correct in shape and coloring — accurate enough for a reference library. One of the foremost Agricultural Colleges selected five best-known breeds of the various animals represented. Then Wards secured photographs of blue Ribbon winners at the international Live Stock Show of 1934..."

CATERPILLAR TRACTOR   MARX   LITHO TIN   MECHANICAL   8" LONG   1936

"Climbs over obstacles and down steep grades — nothing seems to stop its progress. Will pull loads, lumbering along, like a big tractor. Suction cup type rubber treads. Strongly built of metal. Controlled speed, start and stop lever. Clockwork motor. Not Prepaid."

MERCHANDISE TRANSFER WAGON AND HORSE
MARX   LITHO TIN   MECHANICAL   9" LONG

Farm toys sold in great numbers throughout the East and Midwest. They were often distributed through hardware stores, farm implement dealers, and agricultural magazines.

**FORDSON TRACTOR**   ARCADE CAST IRON   6" LONG   1928   79¢
**TWO-BOTTOM PLOW**   ARCADE   5-3/4" LONG   1928   69¢

**McCORMICK-DEERING THRESHING MACHINE**   ARCADE   CAST IRON
12" LONG (FEEDER AND STACKER EXTEND TO 18")   1928

**TOY TEAM WAGON**   RICH TOYS   PAINTED WOOD/STENCIL   35" LONG   1926

Farm wives cooked for gangs of men at threshing time.
Washing the cream-separator was a year-round job.

"A comical toy. Uncanny
how it operates. This mule
has real pep and is some
kicker. He backs up when
he should go forward and
rears up on his hind legs
so that the poor driver
doesn't know what to do."

HEE-HAW    MARX MECHANICAL    LITHO TIN
10-1/4" LONG    1926    43¢

CREAM SEPARATOR WITH BUCKET
ARCADE    CAST IRON    5" HIGH    1932

"Nothing's as
balky as a mule,
but this is the
balkiest of balky
mules! Dog accom-
panies the driver."

JENNY THE BALKY MULE    UNIQUE ART    LITHO TIN    MECHANICAL    9" LONG    1922

"Promenading Porky Pig. Wind him up and this little pig struts along, flipping his hat, twirling his parasol…"

The little pig who doffs his top hat is the first of three versions. This version is the most difficult to find — with or without a hat. In the other two versions Porky simply prances about, spinning his umbrella.

A concealed bellows gives sound to this pig as he rides his hobby horse.

**PUSHY-PIGGY**  FISHER-PRICE  ◎ ◎ ◎ ◎
LITHO PAPER ON WOOD   1932   $1.25

Carved with great detail, the glass-eyed circus and farm animals were some of the earliest the A. Schoenhut Company produced.

**PIG**  SCHOENHUT   PAINTED WOOD WITH GLASS EYES   ◎ ◎ ◎
8" LONG   1920s   PAUL AND KATIE HEDBURN COLLECTION

**PORKY PIG WITH TOP HAT**  ◎ ◎ ◎
MARX   LITHO TIN   MECHANICAL
1941   44¢

"Propelled by motor, this mule walks forward and back. Because he is unregulated, you never know when the mule will step back and forth."

**GO'N BACK MULE**   FISHER-PRICE
LITHO PAPER ON WOOD   MECHANICAL   1931   $1.25

Disney's "Ferdinand" is based on the 1936 children's classic by Munro Leaf. The illustrations are by illustrator Robert Lawson.

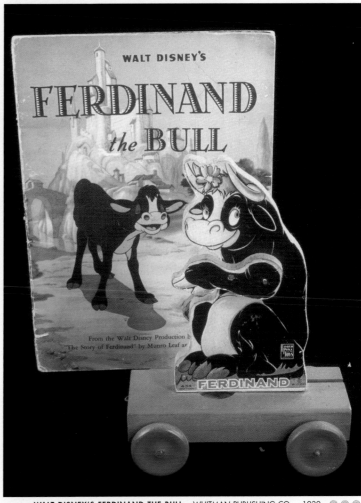

This is an early (bucking) pull-toy not normally associated with the Tinker Toy Company.

**BILLY GOAT**   TINKER TOY CO.   PAINTED WOOD   1928   $1.50

**WALT DISNEY'S FERDINAND THE BULL**   WHITMAN PUBLISHING CO.   1939
**FERDINAND THE BULL**   FISHER-PRICE   LITHO PAPER ON WOOD   1939   44¢

**BABY AND THE GOOSE**   LITHO PAPER ON WOOD   MANUFACTURER UNKNOWN   MID-1920s   ◎ ◎

"Watch the goose wobbling along, bobbing its head up and down trying to shake off the witch and cat."

**PECKING GOOSE WITH WITCH AND CAT**   UNIQUE ART   ◎ ◎ ◎
LITHO TIN   MECHANICAL   8-1/2" LONG   1930s

"Pull this duck and hear him quack! As his beak opens and closes, his body waddles and head wags back and forth."

**SNAPPY QUACKY**   FISHER-PRICE   LITHO PAPER ON WOOD   11" LONG   1950   $2.50
**SNAP-QUACK**   FISHER-PRICE   LITHO PAPER ON WOOD   11" LONG   1947   $1.98

**DADDY DUCKY WADDLE**   HUSTLER TOYS   PAINTED WOOD   1926   47¢   EACH: ◉
**RUBBER SQUEEZE DUCK**   REMPEL MFG. CO   c1930
**DUCK**   CHEIN   LITHO TIN   MECHANICAL   1937   25¢
**AUNTIE DUCK**   TOY KRAFT   PAINTED WOOD AND CARDBOARD   LATE 1920s

"These colorful ducks paddle 'round 'n 'round as their heads move up and down...."

MECHANICAL DUCK(S)   BUFFALO TOYS   PRESSED STEEL   MECHANICAL (FIRST TWO DUCKS)   1948   $1.98

# home (sweet home)

Home is where
the heart is.

– PLINY THE YOUNGER

IN THE EARLY YEARS of the twentieth century, the American middle-class family, with dad at the head, was the backbone of the nation. Americans believed in "The American Way of Life." Living an "ought" culture instead of a "want" culture, they honored and obeyed authority, accepting rules, rituals, and conventions of every aspect of daily life: dress, speech, personal relationships, public behavior, and sexual practices. Chastity was common, divorce and cursing uncommon. Women wore dresses, hats, and gloves, men ties and jackets. Some were better off than others but just about everyone was in the same boat.

Seventy percent of the milk sold in America in 1930 was distributed door-to-door from 12,000 home-delivery dairies by some 70,000 milkmen. As late as the mid-1930s, milk was delivered by horse and wagon (the horse knew the route and stopped automatically at each house). During World War II, the government called on U.S. industries to cut back on the use of gas and manpower. Home delivery service was trimmed, consumers went to food stores for their milk, and when, after the war, supermarkets opened across the country, the milkman (along with ribald milkman jokes) was gone in all but a few areas.

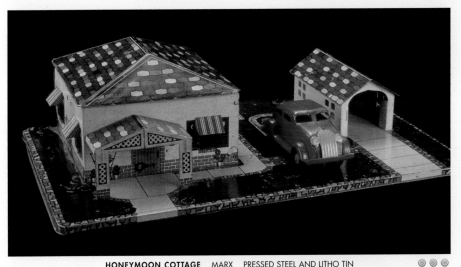

**HONEYMOON COTTAGE**   MARX   PRESSED STEEL AND LITHO TIN
BATTERY LIGHT   1940   89¢
**CHRYSLER AIR-FLOW CAR**   MARX   5-1/2" LONG   PRESSED STEEL   1936   10¢

**GENERAL ELECTRIC REFRIGERATOR**
ARCADE   6" HIGH   1928

This is a very close toy approximation of the General Electric white enameled refrigerator with monitor top.

Born May 28, 1934, the Dionne quintuplets were the most famous babies in the world.

There was cream at the top of the bottle when the milk was delivered each morning.

**TOYLAND'S FARM PRODUCTS MILK AND CREAM WAGON**   MARX   LITHO TIN   MECHANICAL   10" LONG   1931   25¢

MILK WAGON   RICH TOY CO.   18-1/2" LONG   1931   98¢

"When toy is pulled along horse's legs move in a realistic manner...well-built, able to take abuse."

ICE TRUCK   MARX   PRESSED STEEL   13" LONG   1949

MILK FARMS TRUCK   BUDDY 'L   WOOD   13-1/2" LONG   1945   EACH:
MILK TRUCK   KINGSBURY   MECHANICAL   PRESSED STEEL   9" LONG   1936

"A replica of the truck adopted by leading dairies throughout the country for the distribution of milk."

The Divco four-cylinder truck was economical to operate, specifically designed to idle between frequent stops and starts.

> The iceman delivered to your icebox whatever amount your window display card indicated: 25, 50, 75 pounds. If there were kids about, he often chipped off a piece for them.

"...really washes. Take off top, put in doll clothes with soap and water inside. Turning handle moves vacuum cup up and down and squeezes out dirt."

**RED THE ICEMAN** MARX ⦾⦾⦾⦾⦾⦾
LITHO TIN   MECHANICAL   8" HIGH   1935   45¢
DON AND SALLY KAUFMAN COLLECTION

**MICKEY MOUSE WASHING MACHINE**   OHIO ART   8" HIGH   1934   19¢ ⦾⦾⦾

**LITTLE LAUNDRESS**   LAVELLE CO.   1926
**OILCLOTH DOLL**   MANUFACTURER UNKNOWN   1930

LITTLE ORPHAN ANNIE CLOTHES PINS   TRANSOGRAM   1938   19¢

"The loom has two harnesses and the width of the warp space is 4". This makes it possible to weave runners, neckties and a great many other beautiful articles in stripes and checks..."

"Designed for the busy little girl. Outstanding in the practical as well as entertaining and educational value..."

WEAVING LOOM   TRANSOGRAM   1938   19¢

LOOM #60   STRUCTO   PRESSED STEEL   13" HIGH   1920

**DOLLY SEWING SET**   TRANSOGRAM   1937   19¢

▷ This seven-and-one-half-inch doll has movable arms and legs and comes with twelve dresses all cut out and ready to be sewn. A pair of scissors, needles, thimble, thread, yarn, and flowerpots for dolly's house.

"If you are a little girl just learning to handle needle and thimble, you can be a lifesaver to a busy mother by learning to mend. If you are a big girl with a new husband's shirts and socks to take care of, your alertness to his material needs is sure to make a real hit with him..."

Uh-oh. Did something break?

**SWEEPIN' MAMMY**   LINDSTROM   LITHO TIN   MECHANICAL   1930s   ◎ ◎ ◎

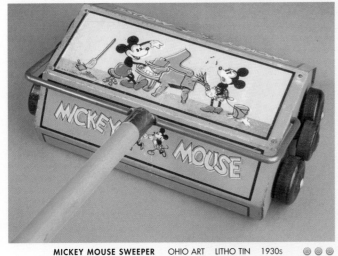

**MICKEY MOUSE SWEEPER**   OHIO ART   LITHO TIN   1930s   ◎ ◎ ◎

▷ Never mind the effectiveness of this sweeper. It's so pretty!

When the toy is pulled along, ◁
the watchdog looks in and out
of his doghouse watchfully.

**WATCHDOG** HUSTLER CO. WOOD AND METAL 1925 89¢ ◎ ◎

**MICKEY MOUSE TEA SET** CHEIN LITHO TIN 1930s 15-PIECE SET 25¢; 21-PIECE SET 42¢ ◎ ◎ ◎

**PASTRY SET** TRANSOGRAM 1930s ◎

Two family pets. The one formal and stiff, the other — the pugilistic one — bobbing his head, is ready for action.

FRAN-ZELL BOW-WOW HUSTLER CO. WOOD 1926 89¢
GROWLEY GROUCH 1926 ALL-FAIR? WOOD 1926 89¢

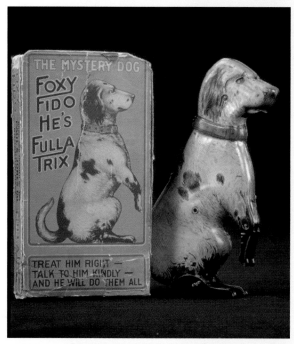

Turn this dog upside down, then upright, and he will sit up straight, open his eyes, and stick out his tongue.

**FOXY FIDO THE MYSTERY DOG** LITHO TIN
PAUL S. JONES CO. 7" HIGH 1924

Self-sustaining, small-town life was the norm in America between the two World Wars, a time of profound quiet, when the distant barking of a dog reminded one of just how quiet things were.

"When pulled you hear loud sniffs — his tail wags and feet move."

**SNOOPY** FISHER-PRICE LITHO PAPER ON WOOD 16" LONG 1938

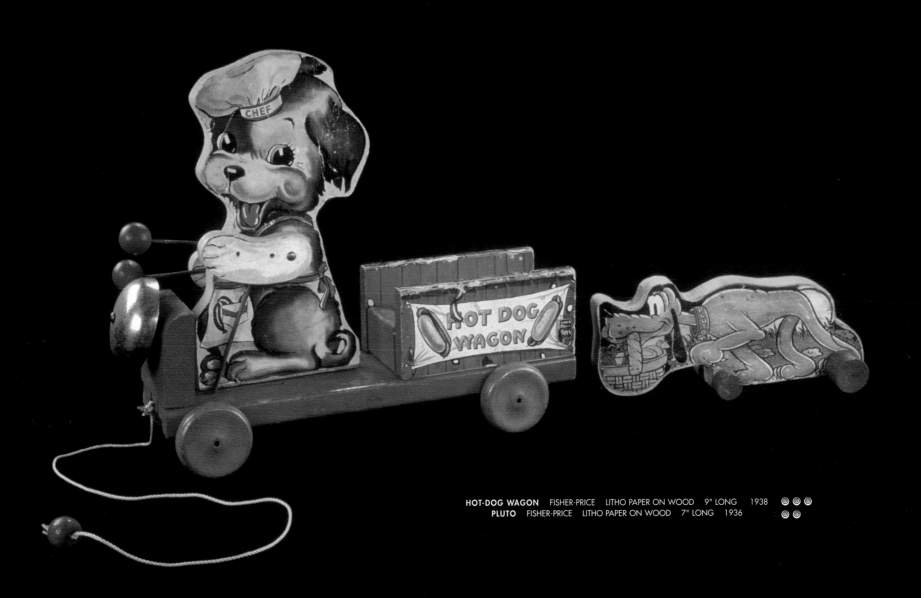

**HOT-DOG WAGON**   FISHER-PRICE   LITHO PAPER ON WOOD   9" LONG   1938
**PLUTO**   FISHER-PRICE   LITHO PAPER ON WOOD   7" LONG   1936

"Kitty's tail is in the air! New simplified mechanism enables the tiniest tot to play with an action toy. Just push lever down. Release and watch Kitty chase ball. Can be repeated continually."

**MYSTERY CAT**   MARX   LITHO TIN   7" LONG   1930s   47¢

An old English game first marketed in the United States at the end of the nineteenth century, Tiddledy Winks was a game one could play alone, with others, or with the family cat.

**COMBINATION TIDDLEDY WINKS GAME**
PARKER BROTHERS   LATE 1920s

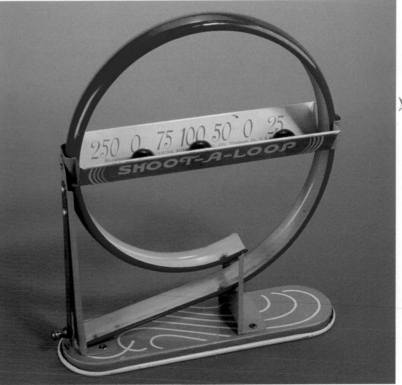

**SHOOT-A-LOOP**   WOLVERINE   LITHO TIN   9" HIGH   1929   25¢

"Plunger shoots marbles around the loop...they'll either fall into the holes numbered from 0 to 250 or run back without scoring. Bright lithographed all metal ramp."

Parlor games were a family pastime. Games such as Pick-Up-Sticks and the Ouija Board were enormously popular. A 1942 survey revealed that 87 percent of Americans played cards.

**1-2-3-4 PICK-UP-STICKS**   O. SCHOENHUT   LATE 1930s

"Provides hours of creative amusement. Everything necessary for painting, coloring pictures, and making drawings."

**TOM SAWYER'S PAINTING SET**
STANDARD SOLOPHONE MFG. CO    EARLY 1930s

1922: Sinclair Lewis writes *Babbitt.*

"52 gloss-finish cards have illustrations of authors or illustrations depicting their work."

**FAMOUS AUTHORS**    RUSSELL MFG. CO.    1922

"Official Boy Scouts Game. Contains several new and original features, one in particular, whereby all players move and play not in turn, but at the same time. The player accumulating the greatest number of honors during the progress of the game is declared the winner. Heavy, handsomely lithographed board shows designs of the different degrees of honor."

**BOY SCOUTS GAME OF PROGRESS**   PARKER BROTHERS   1926   $3

1922: George Gershwin composes *Rhapsody in Blue.*

"The Tell Bell Questioner, with its beautifully pictured cards, questions and conundrums both puzzling and exciting, holds everyone's attention. It is a marvelous toy, one of the greatest educational toys ever. Made in a heavy wooden box, complete with the nature series of 8 beautifully colored cards and 12 printed cards..."

**THE TELL BELL ELECTRIC QUESTIONER**
KNAPP ELECTRIC & NOVELTY CO.   1927   $4.50

At day's end, the family often
gathered in the parlor,
dad read the paper, mom knitted,
the kids entertained themselves.

PUZZLES   A.C. GILBERT   1939   $1.39

"Here's a complete outfit containing 21 fascinating puzzles. Will provide hours of entertainment at social gatherings and parties. Instruction book explains solution of puzzles in detail."

Marbles have been around since the dawn of history. American manufacturers make 350 million marbles a year. In the prewar days when children "knuckling down" outside a ring drawn in the sand challenged each other as to who was the best "shooter," the marbles that counted were Aggies, Black Beauties, Bumboozers, Chalkies, Clearies, Commies, Glassies, Mibs, Peewees, and Shooters.

TOPS, MARBLES, A YO-YO AND A GYROSCOPE

"Kiddie pedals away on his velocipede straight ahead or in circles,
swaying from side to side in an easy natural looking way."

**BOY ON TRICYCLE** UNIQUE ART  MECHANICAL  LITHO TIN  1930s  89¢  ◉ ◉ ◉

"You can go back to the place but never to the time."

– MAXIM

# life in the big city

"Like perfume in an empty room, an old toy speaks to something vital and lingering, something just missed."

– JERRY KNIP

SUNDAYS FOUND AMERICAN TOWNS and streets quiet and almost empty. The sale of goods on Sunday was a violation of the law. "Blue laws" dated from the seventeenth century when ordinances, brought to the American colonies from England governing Sunday behavior, were printed on blue paper. Before World War II, if you needed a bag of flour from the grocery store or a prescription filled at the drug store, you were probably out of luck.

A captivating view of 1927 Main Street America as various vehicles, the size of Cracker Jack prizes, move up and down a generic Main Street in a steady stream of traffic as a policeman and various pedestrians look on.

MAIN STREET   MARX   MECHANICAL   24" LONG   1927

A bagatelle game that reminds town and city
kids to play safely: Stay on the Sidewalk.

**PICKLE TRUCK WITH BATTERY LIGHTS**
METALCRAFT   PRESSED STEEL   10" LONG   1928

**SOS BAGATELLE GAME**   DURABLE TOY & NOVELTY CO.   1947

**COCA-COLA TRUCK**   METALCRAFT   PRESSED STEEL   11" LONG   1928

"The Tricky Taxies are indeed tricky. Wind them up and if they are headed for the edge of the table they will not fall off. Likewise, if you put them next to a water glass or a cigar box, they will continue moving around the object until no more power remains in their little spring motors."

**PLAY STORES**   MARX   LITHO TIN   4-1/2" LONG   1930s   25¢
**TRICKY TAXIES**   MARX   LITHO TIN   4-1/2" LONG   1930s   25¢

EACH: ◎

THE CORNER GROCER   WOLVERINE   LITHO TIN   31" X 14"   1929   $1.39

> The general store and the corner grocery were fixtures in pre-World War II America.

"Go into business with a modern grocery — all metal to stand hard use! Center panel looks like the interior of a store 'bout a block long! Two side sections with three shelves apiece fully stocked with empty miniature packages. Separate refrigerator counter where you sell cold meats, fish, cheese (just pretend of course, they're only painted on!) Counter has white porcelain-like top. Roll of wrapping paper, platform scale with moving weight indicator, miniature French phone, order pad, package of play money are included."

> "Store register combined with a savings bank for real money to be deposited. The bank locks and unlocks automatically and registers each time nickel, dime or quarter is deposited. This toy combines amusement with an educational value."

BENJAMIN FRANKLIN CASH REGISTER
SOUTH BEND TOY MFG. CO.   1926   $1.69

TOY MONEY   WHITMAN PUBLISHING CO.   1930   15¢

**TURNER TROLLEY WITH ELECTRIC LIGHT**  PRESSED STEEL  1930  DUDLEY MADDOX COLLECTION

**CHEIN TROLLEY**  LITHO TIN  9" LONG  LATE 1920s
DUDLEY MADDOX COLLECTION

**DAYTON TROLLEY**  PRESSED STEEL  1920s  DUDLEY MADDOX COLLECTION

> "Looks just like
> a real streetcar!"

**TROLLEY**   WOLVERINE   LITHO TIN   13-3/4" LONG   89¢
**LAMP**   LIONEL

**KINGSBURY TROLLEY**   PRESSED STEEL   MECHANICAL   14" LONG   1927

"With the green color of New
York's Fifth Avenue buses,
this bus is an affirmation of
the Yellow Coach Model Z
bus commonly seen in
New York city." Did double-
decker busses ever travel
state to state?

**INTER-STATE BUS**   STRAUSS   LITHO TIN   MECHANICAL   10-1/2" LONG   1926   $1.25
**CLOCK**   MANUFACTURER UNKNOWN   LATE 1920s.

Tidy Tim of the District Sanitation Commission would today be called a "Sanitation Engineer." But in his day, and before vastly increased traffic and the introduction of mechanical street-sweeping machinery, the Tidy Tims of American cities were ubiquitous. (At the turn of the century, New York City street sweepers wore white uniforms, stood for inspection at morning roll call, and swept some streets five times a day.)

**TIDY TIM**   MARX   LITHO TIN   MECHANICAL   7-1/2" HIGH   1939

**DOUBLE-DECKER BUS** ARCADE ◎ ◎ ◎ ◎ ◎ ◎

CAST IRON  1925  DUDLEY MADDOX COLLECTION

**AMBULANCE** MARX  PRESSED STEEL  MECHANICAL  13-1/2" LONG  1936  98¢ ◎ ◎ ◎

**TELEPHONE POLE** LIONEL  9" HIGH  1935

**POLICEMAN** BRADFORD CO.  LITHO TIN  1914 ◎ ◎

**RR CROSSING SIGNAL** MARX  1934  15¢

**JALOPY** STRAUSS  LITHO TIN  MECHANICAL  1926

**GARBAGE TRUCK** MARX  LITHO TIN  9-1/2" LONG  c1950  DUDLEY MADDOX COLLECTION ◎ ◎

**TRASH BOX** ("KEEP OUR STREETS BEAUTIFUL — DRIVE A BUICK")  MANUFACTURER UNKNOWN  1920

Before World War I, most Americans did not own a car, nor know how to drive. Road signs proclaimed "This is God's country, so don't drive through it like hell."

WRECKER   BUDDY 'L'   PRESSED STEEL   26-1/2" LONG   1928   BRAD CHAPMAN COLLECTION

AMBULANCE   TOOTSIE TOY (SAMUEL DOWST CO.)   POT METAL
3-1/2" LONG   BRAD CHAPMAN COLLECTION

Arcade toys were sold through the Arcade catalog and through 15,000 International Harvester dealers.

INTERNATIONAL HARVESTER RED BABY WRECKER
ARCADE   CAST IRON   10-3/4" LONG   1928   DUDLEY MADDOX COLLECTION

MAN ON BENCH   BARCLAY   2" HIGH   1930s   5¢

WRECKER   WYANDOTTE   LITHO TIN   1950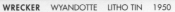

1923: 21 year-old Bobby Jones wins the United States Open golf tournament.

**REPUBLIC LADDER FIRETRUCK**   PRESSED STEEL   1920s
**AHRENS FOX PUMPER**   TURNER TOY CO.   PRESSED STEEL   LATE 1920s   DUDLEY MADDOX COLLECTION

"Always ready for a rescue, Smokey climbs sure-footedly to the top of the ladder, one rung at time."

FIRETRUCK    BUDDY 'L'    PRESSED STEEL    26" LONG    1923
BRAD CHAPMAN COLLECTION

SMOKEY JOE FIREMEN    MARX    LITHO TIN
MECHANICAL    1935    47¢
(ONE FIREMAN AND 23" LADDER)

A motor driven
ladder truck with
ladders operating
automatically when
the truck runs into an
obstruction, rising to
a height of 38 inches.

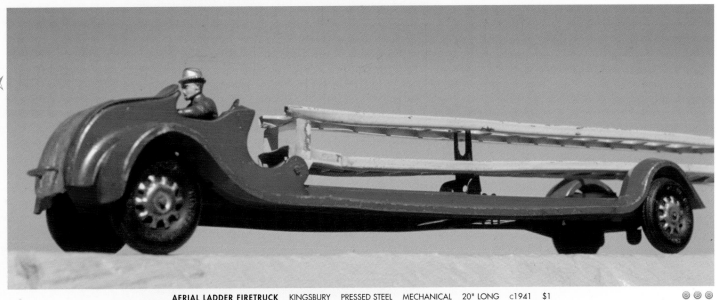

**AERIAL LADDER FIRETRUCK**   KINGSBURY   PRESSED STEEL   MECHANICAL   20" LONG   c1941   $1

In many small towns,
volunteer firemen were on
call to rush to save their
neighbor's house or store.

**KINGSBURY PUMPER**   PRESSED STEEL   25" LONG   1926   DUDLEY MADDOX COLLECTION

**STREET SWEEPER**   NYLINT   PRESSED STEEL   MECHANICAL   1952

**STREET REPAIR TRUCK**   PRESSED STEEL   TONKA   1956
**TOOLS**   ARCADE   CAST IRON   1920s

"Complete telegraph instruments. Sending and receiving. C.W. Buzzer type for communications, flash for night signaling or silent code. High pitch buzzer, bulb, reflector, quick action key. International Morse code charts..."

In 1835, Samuel F. B. Morse demonstrated the first practical use for electricity by transmitting signals from a sending instrument at one end of a wire to a receiver at the other end by interrupting the electrical current in patterns that could be translated into text. Despite the later invention of the telephone, the telegraph, with its punch, brevity and immediacy, was an excellent medium for terse messages:

"NEED $50 STOP SEND SOONEST." "IT'S A GIRL." "WE REGRET TO INFORM YOU..."

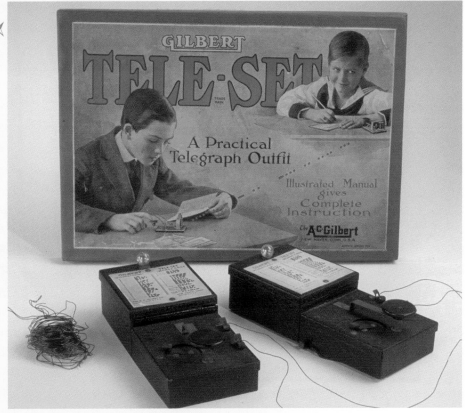

**TELEGRAPH SET**   A. C. GILBERT   1939   $2.50   ◎ ◎

1924: F. Scott Fitzgerald writes *The Great Gatsby*; Adolf Hitler, *Mein Kampf.*

**MICKEY MOUSE TELEPHONE**   N.N. HILL BRASS CO.   PRESSED STEEL   1934   25¢   ◎ ◎ ◎

"Machine prints from metal type (not rubber) on any size paper up to 9 in. wide. There are 40 characters on the dial; complete alphabet in easily read CAPITAL LETTERS, numerals and punctuation marks. Turn dial to the letter you want, press the center lever, and it prints. Spacing lever at side. 3 extra ink rolls included."

**FIVE STAR FINAL GAME**   1930   2¢

**DELUXE TYPEWRITER**   MARX   1932   $2.19   (1935, $1.69)

**U.S. MAIL TRUCK WITH LATTICED SIDES**   STRUCTO   LITHO TIN   15-1/2" LONG

1925: *An American Tragedy*
by Theodore Dreiser is published.

**TOY MAIL BOX**   HULLEO TOYS   LITHO TIN   4-1/2″ HIGH
**SPEED KING**   WYANDOTTE   LITHO TIN   MECHANICAL   1933

**KEEP TO THE RIGHT**   ARCADE   4-1/2″ HIGH   1928
**"CRACKER JACK"**   STRAUSS   LITHO TIN   MECHANICAL   1920
**FUNNY FLIVVER**   MARX   LITHO TIN   MECHANICAL   7″ LONG   1926   43¢

**KID FLYER**    B&R CO.    LITHO TIN    MECHANICAL    9" LONG    1922    DUDLEY MADDOX COLLECTION

Simply lifting up one end of the string will cause these bicyclists to race along. Lifting up the opposite end of the string will cause them to race backwards!

**COLLEGE BOY, POLICEMAN, CHARLIE CHAPLIN, UNCLE SAM** EACH: ◎ ◎ ◎
QUADRIGA TOY CO. FOR AMERICAN FLYER (A.C. GILBERT CO.)    LITHO TIN    8″ LONG

"Ting-a-ling! Santa and his reindeers are coming! Santa pulls the reins — when you've wound the toy up — and the bells ring! A toy that tickles the youngsters."

**SANTEE CLAUS**    STRAUSS    LITHO TIN    MECHANICAL    12″ LONG    1926    89¢    ◎ ◎ ◎

"Toys...captivate the imagination, they give a feel of awe for the wonders of the world.

# america takes to the road

It is hardly worth the effort to try to grow up and live fully with, a world that is not full of wonder."

– BRUNO BETTELHEIM

HENRY FORD'S MODEL T represented the first family car, heralding changes in everything from production techniques to mass-marketing. By 1927 15 million Model Ts had been sold. Giving new meaning to the phrase "mass production," a completed car rolled off the line every 24 seconds.

Any color was available, said Henry Ford, "as long as it was black."

Gas station owners competed for customers by offering giveaways — free maps, balloons for the kids, sets of glassware — but especially by offering good service: washing the windshield, checking the oil and water, air pressure in the tires, the fan belt and even (sometimes) brushing out the carpeting inside the customer's car. All this besides filling the gas tank.

By 1930 there were 26 million cars on the roads. Instead of jumping on and off freight trains, it was easier to "thumb" a ride. Hitchhiking became as American as apple pie. Vagabonds (often women) were seen by many people as victims of the Depression. Picking up a student with his beanie and college sticker pasted on the side of his suitcase, or a soldier hitchhiker during World War II, was a kind of patriotic duty.

Buddy 'L' toys were spot welded and riveted like a real car. They were given two coats of enamel and then baked to give them a hard surface. "Built to Endure," the company claimed their toys would outlast several generations. The front wheels of this Flivver can be turned with the steering wheel.

**FORD FLIVVER COUPE**   BUDDY 'L   PRESSED STEEL   11" LONG   1924   $2.65   ◎ ◎ ◎ ◎

A flywheel on the rear axle causes the rear wheels to spin rapidly. When set on the floor, the car shoots forward several feet by momentum.

**COUPE**   REPUBLIC   PRESSED STEEL   11" LONG   1925   DUDLEY MADDOX COLLECTION   ◎ ◎ ◎

A wonderfully flamboyant car with rumble seat, spare tire, and a spectacular motor ornament.

**ROYAL COUPE** (ALSO CALLED KING RACER)   MARX   LITHO TIN   MECHANICAL   8-1/2" LONG   1925   23¢

STUTZ   MARX   LITHO TIN   MECHANICAL   16" LONG   1929   $1.08   ◎ ◎ ◎

A federal highway numbering system —
even numbers for east-west routes, odd
numbers for north-south routes — was
initiated in 1927, with marker signs on
highways and numerical designations
on maps.

"'Fill her up? Yessir! It's fun
to get 'service' here. Just drive
up to one of two gas pumps and
pretend to fill it — or drive onto
the greasing platform...crank up
the platform — and the electric
light underneath turns on!
(Lights and battery included.)"

With the accessory water can
and portable oil wagon, this toy
reflects an era when air, water,
and maps were free; the attendant
washed your windshield; gas was
seven cents a gallon; and a lunch
counter (are those two lads
Laurel and Hardy in disguise?)
was nearby.

ROADSIDE REST SERVICE STATION   MARX   13"X10"   PRESSED STEEL AND LITHO TIN   1930   $1   ◎ ◎ ◎ ◎

With endless play value, this highly realistic,
1930 three-piece car and gas station set
(stop light not pictured) sold for one dollar.

**GAS PUMPS** MARX LITHO TIN 9-1/2" LONG (BATTERY-OPERATED LIGHTS) EACH: ◎ ◎ ◎
**COUPE** MARX LITHO TIN MECHANICAL 7" LONG

**HERCULES OIL TANKER #500**   CHEIN   LITHO TIN   MECHANICAL   1928   DUDLEY MADDOX COLLECTION   ◎ ◎ ◎ ◎ ◎

1926: First flight of a liquid-propelled rocket.

**KENTON DUMP TRUCK**   CAST IRON   15" LONG   1920s   DUDLEY MADDOX COLLECTION   ◎ ◎ ◎ ◎ ◎ ◎

**REPUBLIC VAN**   PRESSED STEEL   FRICTION   1920s   DUDLEY MADDOX COLLECTION   ◎ ◎ ◎ ◎

Five different body types
could be built from this
set: roadster, coupe,
sedan, van, or racecar.

**AUTO-BUILDER**  SCHOENHUT  WOOD  11" LONG  1929

**BROUGHAM**  KINGSBURY  LITHO TIN  MECHANICAL  14" LONG  1927
**BUICK "NO PARKING" SIGN**  (MAKER UNKNOWN)  DUDLEY MADDOX COLLECTION

**CADILLAC**  MARX  LITHO TIN  MECHANICAL  11" LONG  1931  25¢

Nominally a Cadillac,
this sporty coupe with
adjustable front wheels is
a composite car featuring
a long hood for its big
motor, folding luggage
rack, golf bag compart-
ment, and landaulet bars
on its hardtop.

In 1933, nearly one-quarter of the work force was unemployed. The economic crisis facing the United States was so dire that many people thought democracy might collapse.

**TOWN CAR** KINGSBURY LITHO TIN
MECHANICAL 1927 DUDLEY MADDOX COLLECTION

YELL-O-TAXI STRAUSS LITHO TIN MECHANICAL 8-1/4" LONG 1932

**HOBO**   SCHOENHUT   WOOD AND CLOTH   1915
**HOBO TRAIN**   UNIQUE ART   LITHO TIN   MECHANICAL   1926   48¢

**HOBO**  AMERICAN METAL TOYS  2" HIGH  5¢

There is something about a highway headed west that draws you on.

"Brother, can you spare a dime?"

1926: Gene Tunney upsets Jack Dempsey for the World's heavyweight boxing title. Gertrude Ederle is the first woman to swim the English Channel.

The Joy Riders of the 1920s were not the only people who crashed on Black Thursday, October 24, 1929. Eleven men jumped to their deaths from their skyscraper offices.

**JOY RIDER**  MARX  LITHO TIN  MECHANICAL  1927

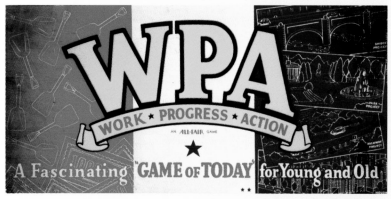

Game title and pieces (paper shovels,
money, chance cards) are based on
the Works Projects Administration,
a federal agency brought into
existence in 1935 to help create jobs
for the masses of unemployed.

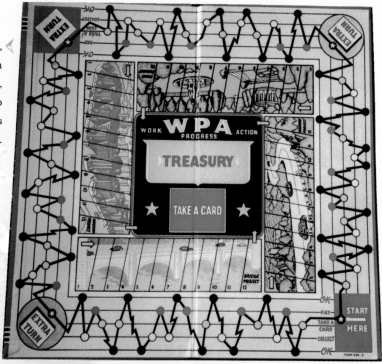

WPA GAME   ALL-FAIR   1935

Hi-Way Henry is taken from Oscar Hitt's comic strip depicting a family on the move (sort of).
When wound, the car shakes and shudders and rears up and down. The dog, his head protruding
from the radiator housing, bobs in and out. The fat lady doesn't sing but listens to the radio
through earphones with a string fastened to the aerial cum-clothesline.

HI-WAY HENRY   NIFTY*   LITHO TIN   MECHANICAL   10" LONG   1927   $1   ◎ ◎ ◎ ◎

*New York distributor George Borgfeldt contracted with the H. Fischer Company in Germany
to manufacture "No name" toys for the American market under the name of "Nifty."

Humphrey was a somewhat obese friend of Joe
Palooka, a comic strip character created by Ham
Fisher in 1927, a heavyweight-boxing champion
with a heart of pure gold. Oddly, no toy was made
of Joe Palooka but this one of his friend peddling
an early homemade version of a mobile home.
This was one of Wyandotte's better toys and
one of the best toys made after World War II.

**HUMPHREY MOBILE**   WYANDOTTE   LITHO TIN   MECHANICAL   1947

**THE GAME OF HITCH HIKER**   PARKER BROTHERS   1930s

CAR CARRIER   GIRARD   PRESSED STEEL   1933

When the sensation of covering vast miles was new and postcards were sent home ("Drove 504 miles today. Yesterday we did 487...") and when gridlock lay far in the future, not everyone could afford a car, or even gas and oil for it.

"Car starts at extreme left end of top runway, speeds through the shaft to the end of that track and then drops onto the next track below. It then runs to the left, drops to third track running to the right and is finally lowered to the bottom runway. Speeding to the end of the track it is then immediately lifted to its top starting point to begin another series of runs and drops. Children marvel at its never-failing stunts."

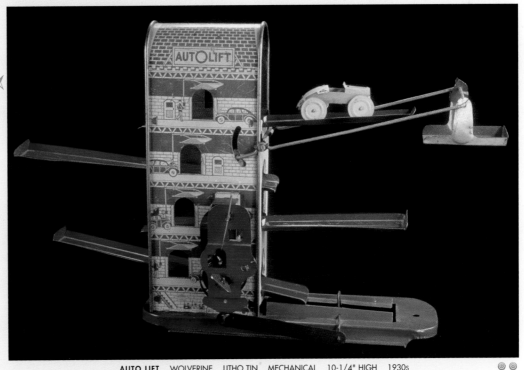

AUTO LIFT   WOLVERINE   LITHO TIN   MECHANICAL   10-1/4" HIGH   1930s

"Daredevil auto speeds down the
upper incline, coasts backwards
down the lower level to where
whirling arms lift it again to the
top of track...to start another spin."

1927: ATT demonstrates "television."

SPEARMINT SEMI-TRUCK   BUDDY 'L'   PRESSED STEEL   24" LONG   1935   $5.98
TRACTOR   STRUCTO   PRESSED STEEL   6" LONG   LATE 1920s
RAILWAY EXPRESS TRUCK   BUDDY 'L'   PRESSED STEEL   25" LONG   1950
RAILWAY EXPRESS TRUCK   MARX   PRESSED STEEL   26" LONG   1949

KEYSTONE RAILROAD EXPRESS TRUCK    PRESSED STEEL    26" LONG    1925    $6.70    ◉ ◉ ◉ ◉

In the early days of the automobile and in the Depression, many men had
to develop their own mechanical skills to avoid expensive repair costs.

1 ◎◎◎
2 ◎◎◎ ◎◎
3 ◎◎◎◎◎
4 ◎◎◎◎◎
5 ◎◎◎◎◎
6 ◎◎◎◎◎
7 ◎◎◎◎
8 ◎◎◎
9 ◎◎◎◎
10 ◎◎

1927: Al Jolson stars in
*The Jazz Singer*, the first talking
motion picture.

FRONT ROW: **BOX TRUCK, TRUCK HAULER, PICKLE TRUCK, SHELL OIL TRUCK, COCA-COLA TRUCK**
BACK ROW: **KROGER VAN TRUCK, MEADOW GOLD CREAMERY TRUCK,**
**WRECKER, PURE OIL TRUCK, DUMP TRUCK**
METALCRAFT   PRESSED STEEL   11" TO 12-1/2" LONG   1928-1933
(IN 1933, A SET OF FOUR PIECES SOLD FOR ONE DOLLAR:
THE TOW, DUMP, AND EXPRESS TRUCKS, PLUS THE STEAM SHOVEL.)

**WRECKER WITH ELECTRIC LIGHTS**   METALCRAFT   PRESSED STEEL   11-1/2 LONG OVERALL   1928   ◎◎◎
**SAND AND GRAVEL TRUCK**   METALCRAFT   11" LONG   1928   ◎◎
**WATER TOWER**   AMERICAN FLYER   LITHO TIN   9" HIGH   1930   $1.25   ◎

**SHELL OIL TRUCK WITH ELECTRIC LIGHTS**  METALCRAFT  PRESSED STEEL  12" LONG  1933  ⊚ ⊚ ⊚ ⊚

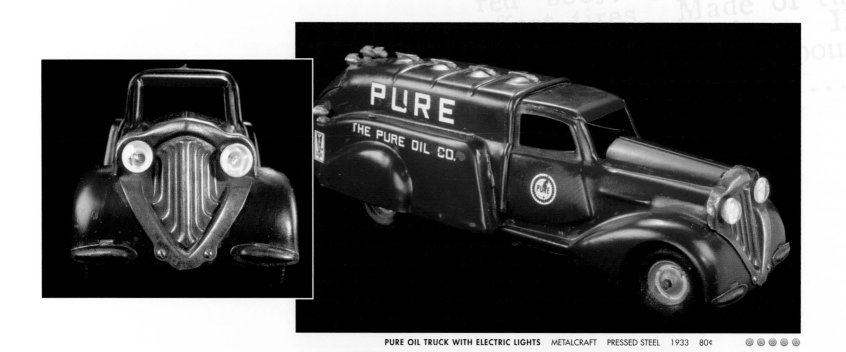

**PURE OIL TRUCK WITH ELECTRIC LIGHTS**  METALCRAFT  PRESSED STEEL  1933  80¢  ⊚ ⊚ ⊚ ⊚ ⊚

"A box contains all parts necessary to build the enameled two-seat Stuz speedster. A separate crank winds a powerful gear-driven, triple-spring, clock-work mechanism."

Billed as an education exercise — "Make Men of Boys!" — this car, with its lowered body, raked windshield, bonnet, and slanted spare tire, was Structo's most elaborate (and expensive) toy.

**DELUXE AUTO BUILDER #12**  STRUCTO  MECHANICAL  PRESSED STEEL  16" LONG  1921  $10

"From one nickle-plated bumper to the other this high-powered car with its electric lights blazing a trail ahead speeds along! Headlights are built into the streamlined body. Wheels have nickeled metal spokes, nickeled radiator grill. Red glass reflector and license plate in rear."

This toy is a virtual replica of Walter P. Chrysler's revolutionary car. Only seven years had elapsed between the 1927 Model T Ford and the ultra-streamlined Chrysler Airflow. Pictured here is the 1937 variance of the first 1934 toy car.

**CHRYSLER AIRFLOW CAR**  KINGSBURY  PRESSED STEEL  MECHANICAL
14-1/2" LONG  1937  98¢  DUDLEY MADDOX COLLECTION

In 1934 Al Capone wrote two testimonial letters to
Henry Ford about the quick getaways of his Ford car.

COUPE   MARX   LITHO-PRESSED STEEL   BATTERY-OPERATED MECHANISM AND ELECTRIC LIGHTS   1930s

"Yes, you can believe your eyes — real lights! The latest coupe with a rumble seat." This toy car came with a "radio" — actually, a concealed music box playing, "I'll Be Loving You Always."

**COUPE WITH ELECTRIC LIGHTS AND LINKAGE STEERING**
KINGSBURY   PRESSED STEEL   MECHANICAL   1927   $2.89 (WITH DRY CELL BATTERY)

Countless cars, like this Cor-Cor Graham created with style and for longevity and permanence, were turned over to "scrap-metal drives" during World War II. Never again would we see such artful, machine-crafted playthings.

**GRAHAM**   COR-COR  CO.
PRESSED STEEL   1932   DUDLEY MADDOX COLLECTION

**SINCLAIR OIL TRUCK**   WYANDOTTE   PRESSED STEEL   c1934

Begun during the war when steel for toy making was scarce, the Buddy 'L'
Company developed these sleek wood toy cars, continuing them after the war until
steel was plentiful once again. The convertible's top can be raised and lowered.

**STATION WAGON** BUDDY 'L' WOOD 19" LONG 1946     EACH: ◎ ◎ ◎
**TOWN AND COUNTRY CONVERTIBLE** BUDDY 'L' WOOD 19" LONG 1947

Manufactured during the Depression at $5,000,
few of these revolutionary real cars were made.

**SCARAB** BUDDY 'L' MECHANICAL 10-1/2" LONG 1936   ◎ ◎ ◎

**CORD** COUPE MODEL 810 WYANDOTTE PRESSED STEEL 13" LONG 1936   ◎ ◎ ◎

The epitome of modernity, the Cord's classic
styling with its "coffin-nose," concealed headlamps,
and wrap-around grille was an amazement, causing
adults to stop and stare and children to wish for
the toy. The toy is propelled by a reverse wind-up-
spring motor: press the toy to the ground while
pushing backwards, then release. Designed by
Gordon Buehrig for the Auburn Automobile
Company and underwritten by the Stoute Motor
Car Corporation, only five of the real cars were
made when, in 1937, E.L. Cord's dream collapsed,
as did the making of the toy cars.

Carmakers outdid themselves restyling their cars, making each successive model different, new and improved; representing them as a vision of an obtainable and desirable future; cars that had an aerodynamic effect, that had an image of freedom; cars with "speed, torque and muscle beneath their hoods — "

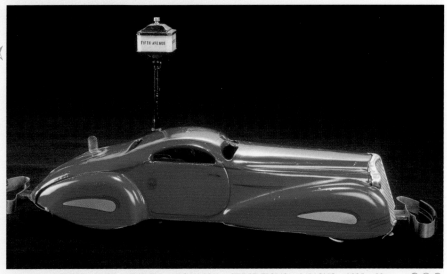

**COUPE**   MARX   LITHO TIN   MECHANICAL   SELF-REVERSING   16" LONG   1935   98¢

"Carries four streamlined cars, measuring 6" long. Equipped with chute or runway which can be pulled down in back for cars on top to slide down. Each of the cars has a wind-up motor; the truck hauler itself does not."

**CAR HAULER**   MARX   PRESSED STEEL   23-1/2" LONG   1935   98¢

"America is the home of toys that educate as well as amuse, that visualize to the boy his future occupations, that start him on the road to construction and not destruction, that...exert the sort of influences that go to form right ideals and solid American character...

# constructing a new century

The American boy is a genuine boy and he wants genuine toys."

– A.C. GILBERT

THE SIMPLICITY AND INTEGRITY of the 1920s to 1950s Late-Industrial Age toys created a miniaturized world easily grasped by children — physically and in their mind's eye.

Toys amuse and distract but they also educate. In the developed world toys become an almost universal part of children's lives. Children, actively involved in making decisions, understand and learn from what they invent, construct, and reconstruct.

In tribal cultures the adults frequently make miniature replicas of the objects they use in their rituals, or in their hunting and warfare, so their children can "play" with them.

Alphabet blocks helped children learn their ABCs, word and picture recognition, and simple construction skills.

**BLOCKS**   MANUFACTURER AND DATE UNKNOWN
**HUMPTY DUMPTY**   OILCLOTH DOLL   MANUFACTURER AND DATE UNKNOWN

1927: Babe Ruth hits 60 home runs.

Each of 30 blocks has different images of animals — each with a name, as well as letters of the alphabet. "Enameled and non-poisonous, the corners are rounded for safety."

**HALSAM SAFETY BLOCKS**   HALSAM   13" LONG   1928   $1

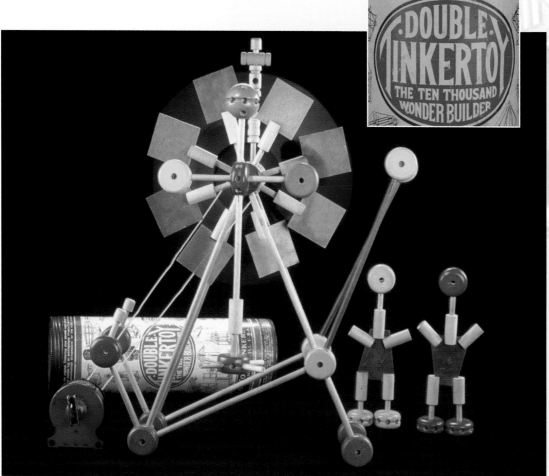

"Child can build windmills, airplanes, cars, by fitting rods into spools and wheels of this simple construction toy. (Very simple in principle being based on the old adage, 'A stick and a spool will amuse a child'.)"

**DOUBLE TINKER TOY WITH MECHANICAL MOTOR**  1926  $1.75

**AMERICAN BRICK BLOCKS**  HALSAM  1930s

GREYCRAFT MODEL TOOLS   GREYCRAFT   1935

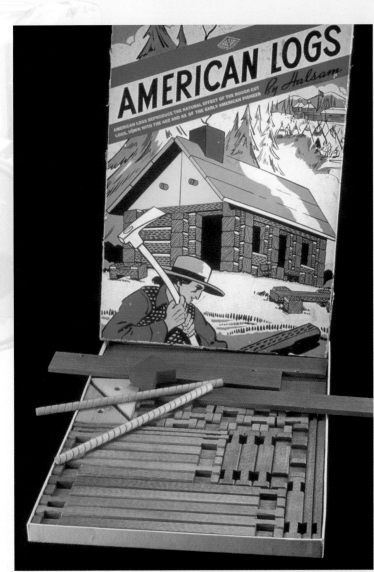

AMERICAN LOGS   HALSAM   1930s

ARCHITECTOR, JR. STONE BUILDING BLOCKS   WENCZEL TILE CO.   1920s

BLACKSMITH    MANOIL    2" HIGH    1934-1942    5 TO 10¢

**INDUSTRIAL COLLAPSIBLE DERRICK** KIDDIES METAL TOYS INC. 1930s
**STEAM SHOVEL** CHEIN LITHO TIN MECHANICAL 1930s
**DERRICK** WOLVERINE LITHO TIN 1930s

**HOME FOUNDRY CASTING SET** HOME FOUNDRY CO. 1939 $1.31

"Smooth out the bumps in the road for your cars! This roller is of heavy cast iron and looks exactly like the ones on the highway."

In 1923, 26,000 miles of new roads were under construction. This 1927 toy was modeled after the real-life Huber Manufacturing Company's steam-powered road roller, heavy machinery that helped revolutionize street and road construction all across America. In 1935, the toy sold for 59 cents.

**ROAD ROLLER** HUBLEY CAST IRON 8" LONG
**HIGHWAY SIGN** ARCADE CAST IRON 1928 10¢

"No springs, no wheels, will run as long as sand is kept in the hopper. See the sand car load up. When filled it swings around in a big circle and the little man dumps it in the can."

1928: *Lady Chatterley's Lover* by D.H. Lawrence is published.

ROAD ROLLER   MARX   LITHO TIN   MECHANICAL   1930s   ◎ ◎ ◎

WOLVERINE "BOWLER ANDY"   LITHO TIN   1920      EACH: ◎ ◎
WOLVERINE SAND CRANE   LITHO TIN   14" LONG   1931
WOLVERINE "BIZZY ANDY"   LITHO TIN   10-1/2" LONG   1929
WOLVERINE "SANDY ANDY"   LITHO TIN   15" HIGH   1929

"The chimney and air pressure whistle serve as the steering mechanism..."

RIDING ROAD ROLLER   KEYSTONE   20" LONG   1931   $7 (1933, $2)   ◎ ◎ ◎

The completion of the Panama Canal in 1914 was one of the great engineering feats of all time, a monumental and unprecedented achievement. For children in 1919 the "Panama" Pile Driver echoed that achievement. There is a lot of spirited action and interaction with this toy as the man speeds up and down, up and down, working, working, working... A simple toy, but one of the great toys.

"Watch the little man handle pile driver. He rides up and down in two-wheel car, working the dummy hammer up and down as long as marbles are kept in hopper above."

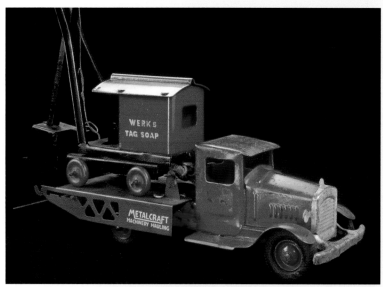

**STEAM SHOVEL TRUCK HAULER**   METALCRAFT   1928   ◎ ◎ ◎ ◎ ◎

**PANAMA PILE DRIVER**   ◎ ◎ ◎
WOLVERINE   LITHO TIN   15" HIGH   1919   $1.17

"It looks and works just like a real steam shovel you often see in building roads or excavating for buildings. Rolls along on heavy corrugated rubber treads. Will push or pull heavy loads up and down hills and inclines without any effort. Powerful shovel will lift heavy loads and can be raised or lowered by turning crank and dumped by a pull of the cord. Cabin is mounted on a turntable..."

**STEAM SHOVEL**   MARX   MECHANICAL   15" LONG OVERALL   1930   ◎ ◎ ◎

**CATERPILLAR TRACTOR SET**   ANIMATE TOY CO.   TIN   1920s   ($3.19 IN 1932)   ◎ ◎ ◎

▷ "This wonderful tractor climbs just as irresistibly as the big tractors you see. The attachments consist of a Snowplow, Sweeper, Scraper, Scoop and Dump cart. With this outfit the boy can do the same things as the men on the big tractors."

1929: Collapse of the U.S. stock market precipitates worldwide economic collapse.

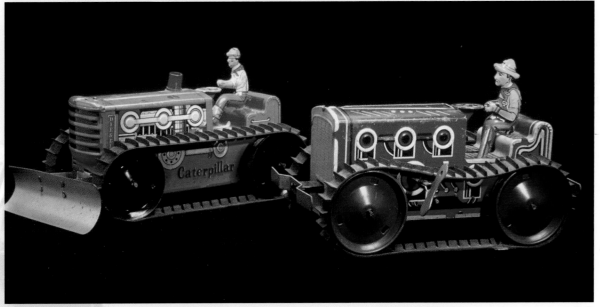

**CATERPILLAR TRACTORS**   MARX   MECHANICAL   LITHO TIN   8" LONG   1930s-1940s   ◎ ◎

CATERPILLAR TRACTOR   MARX   LITHO TIN   11"   1930s-1940s

"This Tractor is built with an especially constructed super-power clock-work motor, making it possible to pull very heavy loads many times its own weight and capable of climbing a very steep grade. Has two gearshifts, one to start and stop, the other to shift for running forward or backward. It is also possible to leave the motor running in neutral position without the Tractor being in action."

"Wind it up and the truck shoots back and forth, up and down — from one mine to the other."

BUSY MINERS   MARX   MECHANICAL   16" LONG   1939   45¢

"When marbles are placed in the tower, Car No. 1 speeds up incline while Car No. 2 races down opposite incline to deposit marble, then rises rapidly up again, and so on. Fast action."

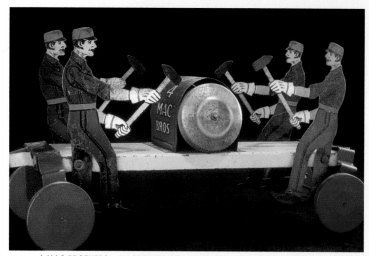

**4 MAC BROTHERS**    MACDOWELL CO.    TIN LITHO    12" LONG    1926    ◎ ◎ ◎

**ELEVATOR SAND TOY**    OHIO ART    TIN LITHO    10" HIGH    1929    ◎ ◎

**NO. 6 OIL WELL SAND TOY**    MACDOWELL CO.    11" HIGH    1927    ◎ ◎
**MARX TRUCKS**    5-1/2" LONG    1934    10¢ EACH    ◎

> "Accurate miniature of real mixer. Put sand and cement in big scoop as it rests on ground and fill water tank on top of mixer. Turning crank raises scoop and sand. Cement and water are poured into the revolving drum and mixed into concrete."

**CEMENT MIXER**   BUDDY 'L'   17" X15"
13 POUNDS   1926   $11.98   FRANK MONTELEONE COLLECTION

1930: The face of George Washington is carved from Mt. Rushmore by Gutzon Borglum.

**HERCULES READY MIXED CONCRETE TRUCK**   CHEIN   LITHO TIN   15" LONG   1929   DUDLEY MADDOX COLLECTION

GILBERT GLASS BLOWING SET    A.C. GILBERT CO.    18" X 10"    1939    $2.25

> "Contains all the essential equipment for real glass blowing. 31 pieces of glass tubes, equipment and apparatus including a constant self-generating alcohol blow torch and 64-page manual showing how to do 80 experiments in glass blowing including how to build a submarine, siphons, etc."

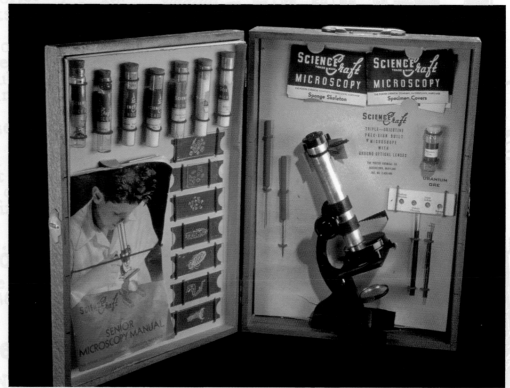

SCIENCE CRAFT MICROSCOPE SET    PORTER CHEMICAL CO.    $6.54

GILBERT CHEMISTRY SET   A.C. GILBERT CO.   1940   $15

> "This unrivaled outfit is the finest set for the student or your scientist. Includes chemicals, apparatus and equipment with 4 big manuals in chemistry, glass blowing, mineralogy and chemical magic. Also scales, beaker, flask, alcohol lamp, generator, thermometer. Wood cabinet has over 9 feet of shelf room and test tube racks. Performs over 800 experiments, many never before offered. Dry Ice, refrigeration, ethyl gas lacquers, electro-chemistry, electro-plating, electrotyping, etc."

GILBERT PHYSICS SET   A.C. GILBERT CO.

GILBERT ELECTRIC EYE SET   A.C. GILBERT CO.   1939   ELECTRIC EYE   $5.50

> "Mysteries of electrical action through Selemium Cell and Sensitive Relay... All experiments illustrated and explained in manual. Basis of action through light rays penetrating Selemium Cell which is extremely sensitive to change of light, either to greater or less conductivity..."

**TIP-TOP PORTER**   STRAUSS   LITHO TIN   MECHANICAL   1919   45¢

Four different sets available: the 89-cent set has 70 parts and builds
100 models; the $8.98 set has 730 parts and builds 600 models.

"Completed models...are substantial structures that you can carry about.
When you tire of one building, pull it apart in a jiffy and start another."

"Just as the Child Builds the Toy, So the Toy Builds the Child"

"Cut a trail through the snow in winter...
in the summer build new roads in your
sand pile! Haul in wrecked autos with the
detachable derrick. The tractor lumbers up
steep 'hills' and over obstacles on its
rubber caterpillar treads."

**CATERPILLAR TRACTOR**   MARX   LITHO TIN   MECHANICAL
(WITH A TRAILER AND CHAIN, THIS 5-PIECE SET SOLD IN 1938 FOR $1.69)

**BILT E-Z THE BOY BUILDER**   SCOTT MFG. CO.
1926   DUDLEY MADDOX COLLECTION

# down to the river
# and the sea

"Nature wants
children to be children
before they are men."

– DR. BENJAMIN SPOCK

THE ATTRACTION OF WATER — river, lake, the sea —
is ever present in us. The fantasy of travel,
speed, leisure, heroism —  young or old,
we find it in those things related to water,
whether by man's hand or nature's.

Unlike handmade ship models, these toy boats
were manufactured to be played with. They are
relatively scarce (especially in good condition)
for the same reason real boats have shorter lives
than other modes of transportation — they are
subject to rust and, alas, Davy Jones's locker.

**PELICAN** CHEIN LITHO TIN MECHANICAL 5-1/4" HIGH 1930s
**SALT WATER TAFFY BOX** KEP & LANE 1930s
**ROWBOAT** MARX LITHO TIN 1930s
**LIGHTHOUSE** MARX LITHO TIN BATTERY-OPERATED LIGHT 1930s
**BARNACLE BILL** CHEIN LITHO TIN MECHANICAL 6-1/4" HIGH 1930s

**PENGUINS** CHEIN LITHO TIN MECHANICAL 3-3/4" HIGH 1936 19¢
**TURTLE WITH BOY** CHEIN LITHO TIN MECHANICAL 6" LONG 1930s 19¢

**NATIVE ON ALLIGATOR** CHEIN LITHO TIN MECHANICAL 15" LONG 1937 24¢

➤ This toy is a take-off on postcards of the period portraying a child, usually a blond girl or an African-American boy, riding an alligator.

"Well, if it isn't the comic Popeye using all that energy of his actually rowing his rowboat. Hand cranked, long running motor keeps Popeye's arms from tiring. Removable oars."

**POPEYE IN ROWBOAT**   HOGE MFG. CO.   LITHO TIN AND PRESSED STEEL   MECHANICAL   15" LONG   1934   $1.75

SKIPPER SAM   FISHER-PRICE   8" LONG   1934   $1   ⊚⊚⊚⊚⊚⊚

▷ "Realistic rowing
action as the toy
is pulled along.
Oars can be
placed in boat."

STEAMBOAT PULLTOYS   MFG. UNKNOWN   LITHO TIN
10" LONG; 14" LONG   1930s   ⊚⊚⊚
⊚⊚⊚

"Walking beam moves up and down as boat travels, bell rings with
a ding-dong. Motor guaranteed against mechanical imperfections." ◁

"SANDY ANDY" FERRY   WOLVERINE   LITHO TIN   MECHANICAL   14" LONG   1920   ⊚⊚⊚

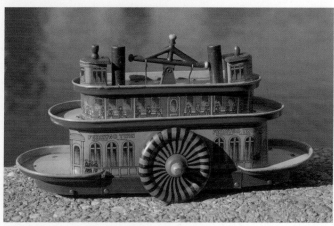

FERRYGO TWIN (PULLTOY)   MFG. UNKNOWN
LITHO TIN   14" LONG   1930S   ⊚⊚⊚⊚

**TURTLE AND RIDER**  CHEIN  LITHO TIN  MECHANICAL  1930s
**SAIL·A·WAY**  STRAUSS  LITHO TIN  MECHANICAL  1924

"Features include Life preserver, real
compass with magnetic needle, cabin with
colored running lights, deck capstan, brass
rails and pulleys, brass wheel, spreader,
movable pennants, leaded keel."

**SLOOP SAILBOAT**  MANUFACTURER UNKNOWN  20" LONG HULL; MAST 26-1/2" HIGH

**JACKEE, THE HORNPIPE DANCER**
STRAUSS   LITHO TIN   MECHANICAL   1924   ◎ ◎ ◎

"Sailor dances as
boat moves forward."

A handsome art deco
style target game from
the early thirties. The
goal is to cause one of
the three sailors to
stand up and salute by
successfully tossing a
rope ring onto a hook.

**QUOITS-AHOY!**   AMERICAN TOY WORKS   32" HIGH   EARLY 1930s   ◎ ◎ ◎

1931: Hoagy Carmichael composes *Stardust.*

Battleship, aircraft carrier, cruiser,
destroyer, submarine, submarine

**KEYSTONE VICTORY BATTLE FLEET**   KEYSTONE TOY CO.   WOOD   22" TO 12" LONG   1930s-1940s   $1.00 – $1.10   ◎ ◎ ◎ ◎

"Battleship launches plane by spring concealed in deck. Minute detail — cabin, mast, pendants, side and headlights and anti-aircraft guns."

**B22 U.S. BATTLESHIP WITH SPRING-LOADED AIRPLANE CATAPULT**

"Submarines fitted with high speed spring-loaded torpedoes, side lights, guns and separate target ships. Timely action for every boy."

**U18 U.S. SUBMARINE**
**U.S. SUBMARINE**

EACH:

"This sleek life-like sub 'speeds along the surface,' then dives only to break through
the surface just like a real sub, then dives again and resurfaces once more...
Movable fins at the bow and rudder at the stern determine depth and direction."

**SUBMARINE**  WOLVERINE  PRESSED STEEL  MECHANICAL  11" LONG  1940  ◎ ◎ ◎

Beautifully made but somewhat expensive boat set for small children. (Or maybe not so small.)

**TILLICUM NATIONAL DEFENSE SET**   MILTON BRADLEY CO.   WOOD   1940s   $4.50

1932: General Douglas MacArthur fires on ex-American soldier "bonus marchers."

This toy ship, like other Orkin ships, was modeled after existing U.S. Navy ships. It has a radio mast, searchlights, large and small caliber guns, four revolving gun turrets. An exceptionally strong steel spring motor turns twin screws.

**B-2 BATTLESHIP**   ORKIN   PRESSED STEEL   MECHANICAL   37" LONG   1929

"Sparkling battleship. Wind up the strong spring motor and watch this 'super-dreadnought' roll across the floor into action. Shoots harmless sparks from 2 long-range guns. Bombs and a bomb catapult that really works, are on deck."

**USS WASHINGTON BATTLESHIP**   MARX   LITHO TIN   MECHANICAL   14" LONG   1930s   25¢

The strong motor of this aircraft carrier turns twin screws. Liberty Playthings boats were supplied with detachable wheels so that they could be brought indoors and played with as floor toys.

**AIRCRAFT CARRIER WITH FOUR CAST-IRON AIRPLANES**
LIBERTY PLAYTHINGS   WOOD   MECHANICAL   28" LONG   1935

"This boat has the capability of launching torpedoes (spring action)."

**DESTROYER TORPEDO BOAT**
LIBERTY PLAYTHINGS   WOOD   MECHANICAL   22" LONG   1935

This freighter, which accurately replicates the freighters sailing the
Great Lakes, has eight separate platform doors that can be slid open,
allowing just about anything to be loaded and transported in it.

**FREIGHTER**   LIBERTY PLAYTHINGS   WOOD   MECHANICAL (MOTOR TURNS TWIN SCREWS)   26" LONG   1931

**FREIGHTER**  KEYSTONE  WOOD  11" LONG  1930s

**TUG BOAT**  BUDDY 'L'  PRESSED STEEL  28" LONG
1928  FRANK MONTELONE COLLECTION

Driven by a compressed air motor and tank
below deck, the Tug Boat was tested by the
original Buddy 'L' (Lundberg) and his father,
the boat's manufacturer, by sending it across
the Mississippi River
at Moline, Illinois.

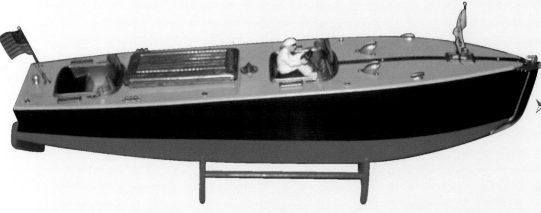

An example of but one of the
impressively built Orkin boats.

**SPEEDBOAT**  ORKIN  PRESSED STEEL  MECHANICAL  18" LONG  1920s-1930s

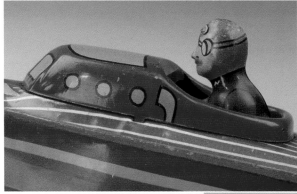

Trailing their miniature wakes, the pleasure ◁ that these windup boats gave their various young owners is inestimable. Has not each child grown up to wish that he could find that wonderful tin boat he used to have? So many years ago? Years that seem like yesterday?

**LINDSTROM SPEEDBOAT**  LITHO TIN  MECHANICAL  13" LONG  1930s AND EARLY 1940s
**LINDSTROM SPEEDBOAT**  LITHO TIN  12" LONG W/MECHANICAL OUTBOARD
**LINDSTROM BABY L SPEEDBOAT**  LITHO TIN  MECHANICAL  10" LONG
**LINDSTROM SPEEDBOAT**  LITHO TIN  MECHANICAL  7" LONG

**LINDSTROM SPEEDBOAT**  LITHO TIN  MECHANICAL  14" LONG

SPEEDBOAT   LINDSTROM   MECHANICAL   1930s

1934: The Dionne Quintuplets are born in Canada.

SPEEDBOAT   LIONEL   17" LONG   1936   $2.50

A powerful and well-made speedboat.
Did Lionel set out to copy the speedboat in
which Gar Wood smashed the 1935 speedboat
racing record? One supposes that Lionel did
indeed — and did it very well too.

SPEEDBOAT #44   LIONEL   17" LONG   1936   $2.50

"A toy is given to a child
from a parent as an expression
of love and caring. The child
holds in his hands that toy
and understands,

on the atcheson, topeka
and the sante fe

without the bother of
words, be it birthday or
Christmas or neither
that he is loved."

– ROBERT LESSER

LIKE DOLLS, trains are a toy category unto themselves. Pictured here are those trains and related railroad toys that were featured in Wards, Sears, Spiegel, and other catalogs — toys that laid no claim to being models of real trains but were charming and toy-like, with unending play-value. To the child who played with these toy trains, they were the real thing.

The development of the American railroad system, joining the east and west coasts at Promontory, Utah, in 1869, affected every aspect of the American economy, from the distribution of manufactured goods to the ease of fast, scheduled travel. All of which was reflected, both seriously and comically, in American toy trains.

The enormous and immediate success of the elaborately lithoed wind-up Mickey Mouse train, with Mickey furiously shoveling coal from the tender in rhythm to a ringing bell, is credited with saving the Lionel Corporation from bankruptcy.

**MICKEY MOUSE TRAIN WITH CARDBOARD CIRCUS TENT**   LIONEL   LITHO TIN (COMPOSITION MICKEY)   1935  ◎ ◎ ◎ ◎

**MICKEY MOUSE HANDCAR** LIONEL
PRESSED STEEL (COMPOSITION FIGURES) MECHANICAL 7" LONG 1935 94¢

**"CHOO-CHOO LOCAL"** FISHER-PRICE LITHO PAPER ON WOOD 1936 49¢

**POPEYE EXPRESS** MARX LITHO TIN MECHANICAL 9" DIAMETER 1934 59¢

"Union Pacific train circles about with
Olive Oyl, Wimpy, Sappo and Sweet Pea
as Popeye flies overhead."

"'Well blow me down' it's the popular cartoon character speeding around on a handcar! While Popeye easily pumps one-handed, poor Olive Oyl needs to eat some spinach!"

**POPEYE HANDCAR**   *MARX*   PRESSED STEEL (RUBBER FIGURES)   MECHANICAL   6" LONG   1935   94¢

"When wound the trolley moves forward in a rocking motion. After advancing a few feet, it stops and begins shaking again, then moves forward as the motorman 'Skipper' desperately manipulates the controller."

**TOONERVILLE TROLLEY**  NIFTY
LITHO TIN   MECHANICAL   6-3/4" HIGH   1923   $1   ◎◎◎◎◎

"Here is by far one of the most unique train sets ever designed. There is nothing on the market to compare with it. Has 10 cars, each one bearing a different military unit. Each car can be detached and has its own individual play value. For example: the tank car has its own sparking action, the large Siege gun mounted on a swivel actually shoots the shells contained in another car, etc...."

**ARMY SUPPLY TRAIN** (ELECTRIC)   ◎◎◎◎◎◎
MARX   LITHO TIN   82" OVERALL   1939   $12

**JOY LINE FREIGHT TRAIN**   GIRARD   LITHO TIN   1934   $1.39

**BUNNY EXPRESS**   LITHO TIN   GIRARD   1927   $1.39

This is not a benign toy.
As the Red Cap pushes the
steamer trunk, a bulldog
jumps out of the trunk
to harass him.

**RED CAP PORTER**   STRAUSS   LITHO TIN   MECHANICAL   1926   48¢ ◎◎◎

**GOLDEN STATE LIMITED**   MILTON BRADLEY CO.   1930s   ◎

Keying on the public's
attraction to the
"streamlining" of
railroad engines, this
beautifully lithographed
game was offered
by the Rexall Drug
Company in 1936 as
a premium for buying
one of its products.

**STREAMLINED TRAIN GAME**   ◎◎
MANUFACTURER UNKNOWN

"With handle bar for steering control the youngster can steer while sitting on the train engine and play indoors and outdoors without tracks. Space in coal tender to pile articles."

**LOCOMOTIVE**   KEYSTONE   PRESSED STEEL   28" LONG   1931   $9.50 (1941, $5.95)

# the sky's the limit

"Man is in love and
loves what vanishes.
What more
is there to say?"

– W.B. YEATS

FROM THE FIRST POWERED AIRCRAFT FLIGHT by the Wright brothers on December 17, 1903, through development of fighter planes for use in World War I, aircraft design steadily advanced. In 1920, transcontinental airmail service was initiated, followed six years later with the first passenger service.

But it was on May 20 and 21, 1927, interest in aviation accelerated worldwide. Neither the world nor 25-year-old airmail pilot Charles Augustus Lindbergh, flying nonstop from Roosevelt Field, New York, to Le Bourget, Paris, in his Ryan "Spirit of St. Louis" monoplane in 33½ hours, would ever be the same.

Many years ago, when you heard the drone of an airplane, you ran out the door to see what kind of aircraft it was. Even in the 1950s, the whole family would pile in the car and drive to the airport just to watch the shiny, sleek planes — the DC-3s and then the DC-4s — every hour or so, taking off and landing, the stairway pushed up to the plane and the passengers stepping down smartly to the tarmac, waving to waiting friends and relatives. It simply was romantic watching it — no question. But it was inspirational, too. What you were seeing and feeling was really special.

After the New York to Paris flight of "Lucky Lindy" (Charles Lindbergh), toy airplanes were sold by the hundreds of thousands, not only in America but around the world.

**SPIRIT OF ST. LOUIS AIRPLANE** METALCRAFT 1929 11" WINGSPAN

**LINDBERGH AIRPLANE** PRESSED STEEL WYANDOTTE 12" WINGSPAN c1930

**CHARLES LINDBERGH DOLL** (GENERIC BABY DIMPLES FACE)    EFFENBEE MFG. CO.    1927
**WE**    G. P. PUTNAM'S SONS    1927

**EAGLE AIR SCOUT AIRPLANE**   MARX   26" WINGSPAN   1923   $1.10   ◎ ◎ ◎

➤ "Push the airplane and the propeller spins!"

**SPIRIT OF ST. LOUIS**   ◎ ◎ ◎ ◎ ◎
UNITED ELECTRICAL MFG. CO.   LITHO TIN AND PRESSED STEEL
19-1/2" HIGH   c1929   PHIL SANDLER COLLECTION

**"SPIRIT OF ST. LOUIS" AIRPLANE AND HANGAR** (CONSTRUCTION TOY)   ◎ ◎ ◎
METALCRAFT   1929   (175 PARTS , $2.59; 260 PARTS, $4.48)

➤ "Lindy Did It! — but more remains to be accomplished. We turn to the youth of the land for the new ideas, which will place aviation on a really practical basis. An educational toy, such as this, may prove to be the starting point for the next great development. Your Son or Daughter may find the answer to some of the problems still facing aviation..."

SPIRIT OF COLUMBIA AIRPLANE  AMERICAN FLYER
LITHO TIN  MECHANICAL  19-1/2" WINGSPAN  1929  $2  ◎ ◎ ◎

"Air Mail is Socially Correct"
poster issued by the
U.S. Postal Service in 1929.

One of the most impressive cast iron toys ever made.
It is heavy, rare, and, as you might guess, today it is expensive.

**AMERICA TRI-MOTOR AIRPLANE**  HUBLEY  ◎ ◎ ◎ ◎ ◎ ◎
CAST IRON  17" WINGSPAN  1928  DAN DAVIS COLLECTION

1935: A miniature golf craze
sweeps the nation.

"Watch plane as it starts from the floor, gathers up speed, and rises high and circles around the building and then — Oh! Just see it loop the loop, right itself, circle around again and whee! There she goes again, looping the loop until it gradually glides down and makes a landing as gracefully as a real plane."

This toy with its suggestive tower was sold three years before the Empire State Building — the highest building in the world — was constructed. (Perhaps Marx peeked at the plans.)

**CAPITAL CITIES AIR DERBY GAME**   ALL-FAIR   1929   ◉ ◉ ◉

**TRAVELING AIRPLANE**   TURNER   ◉ ◉ ◉ ◉ ◉
PRESSED STEEL   24" WINGSPAN   1930   DUDLEY MADDOX COLLECTION

**DARE DEVIL FLYER**   MARX   LITHO TIN
MECHANICAL   SKYSCRAPER: 10-1/2" HIGH
PLANE: 6-3/4" LONG   1928   89¢
◉ ◉ ◉ ◉ ◉

U.S. MAIL AIRPLANE   MARX   LITHO TIN   MECHANICAL   13-1/2" WINGSPAN   1935   47¢

TRI-MOTOR U.S. MAIL AIRPLANE   KEYSTONE TOY CO.
24" WINGSPAN   PRESSED STEEL   1933   $4.50

> This great airplane, with doors that swing out on each side to receive mail, has rapid-fire motors with pistons that move up and down causing a "clicking" noise that suggests roaring down the runway. The steady hum of flight?

"Ask the boy who owns a Keystone"

CITY AIRPORT WITH AIRPLANES (BATTERY-OPERATED LIGHTS) ◉ ◉ ◉
WYANDOTTE  LITHO TIN AND PRESSED STEEL    15" X 11"    1934    $1.75

▷ "An airport that will fill a real need of any young, air-minded child."

This toy is a delight just to look at. Perfectly proportioned, gorgeously yet appropriately lithographed, it has a windsock, dual hangars, dual warning lights, a Ticket Office, Radio Station, Weather Bureau, Dispatcher's Office, Repair Shop. On the back side, a Waiting Room, Restaurant, Drug Store, Newsstand, and an American Airlines, Inc. sign: "Largest Airline in the United States — Serving 57 Principal Cities"

"It's no end of fun watching this realistic aeroplane!
When the motor is wound it gradually rises and flies
level with the top of the tower. When the motor dies
down it glides gracefully to the ground."

Noisy and sluggish, the China Clipper began service in
1936 providing "luxury" travel from San Francisco to Hawaii,
a 2,400 mile hop, flying onward to the Far East.

**CHINA CLIPPER**   CHEIN   LITHO TIN   MECHANICAL   1939   ◎ ◎ ◎
(THE PONTOONS OF THIS AIRPLANE ARE MISSING)

1936: African-American Jesse
Owens wins four gold medals
at the Berlin Olympics.

**AIRPLANE BEACON**   A.E. RITTENHOUSEN CO.   9" HIGH
**CROSS-COUNTRY FLYER**   MARX
LITHO TIN   19" HIGH   6" AIRPLANE   5" ZEPELLIN   1929   ◎ ◎ ◎ ◎

An unusual airplane toy in which a Zeppelin-shaped weight, attached by lines to a rod and two airplanes, causes the planes to take off, fly about, and land as the "zep" moves by gravity down an upright pole.

**NEWTON AERO CIRCUS**

**PONTOON BOAT**  CHEIN  LITHO TIN  MECHANICAL  8" WINGSPAN  1941

**CONSOLIDATED CATALINA PBY MODEL AIRPLANE KIT**  JOE OTT MODEL AIRPLANE CO.  1940s
**CONSOLIDATED CATALINA PBY AIRPLANE**  STROMBECKER  PRE-CUT SOLID WOOD  1930s TO 1940s

It took about two weeks to make a Flying Tiger P-40, a British Spitfire, or a German Messerschmitt: cutting out with a razor blade the rib patterns from the printed sheets of balsa wood, fitting them over the schematics, pinning them down, gluing them with Duco wood cement, waiting overnight for them to dry. And when the body, wings, the tail, and the rudder were each finished, you assembled them, added the rubber band motor, the prop and the wheels, carefully added its tissue paper skin, painted it, added the decals and, finally, holding the airplane lovingly in hand, stood back and admired it, proud of your handiwork. Really proud.

The new-fangled "Autogyro" made its first appearance in 1923. It amazed the public. "It looks like a spider!"

**AUTOGYRO**   WYANDOTTE   PRESSED STEEL   1935

Pulled or pushed, a small child could ride on the Steelcraft zeppelin.

The real Graf Zeppelin was launched in Germany in 1928. It was the predecessor of the doomed Hindenberg that crashed at Lakehurst, New Jersey, in 1937.

**ZEPPELIN**   STRAUSS   TIN OR ALUMINUM   MECHANICAL   9" LONG   c1928
**GRAF ZEPPELIN**   STEELCRAFT   30" LONG   1929   $2.19

Schoenhut also made auto and boat put-together wood sets. But the Dirigible Builder set — the tactile caress of its wood still felt in his hands as the zep floats serenely above the child-builder's bed — is surely the most sublime of all.

"Your own designs as well as those shown in instruction book can be built. Parts are rust proof metal pieces making natural looking ships. Has over 60 large parts and over 300 nuts and bolts. Not intended to fly."

**DIRIGIBLE BUILDER SET**   SCHOENHUT   WOOD   21" LONG   1929
**DIRIGIBLE BUILDER SET**   METALCRAFT   PRESSED STEEL
21" LONG   1929   $1.98

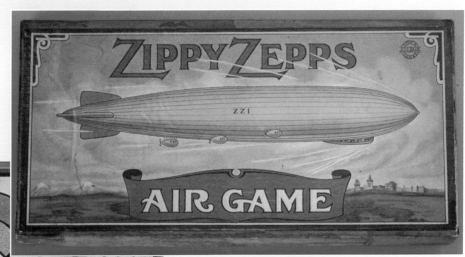

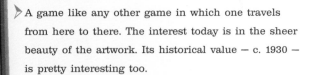

**ZIPPY ZEPPS GAME**   ALL-FAIR

A game like any other game in which one travels from here to there. The interest today is in the sheer beauty of the artwork. Its historical value — c. 1930 — is pretty interesting too.

Representing mastery over distances and the elements and the focus of pride in a nation's achievements, the zeppelin resting at its moorings or flying overhead like a great floating dreamship was a dramatic, never-to-be-forgotten sight.

Designed in 1936, 11,000 Douglas DC-3s would be sold. The most successful commercial aircraft ever built, DC-3s are still flying throughout the world.

**FLYING THE UNITED STATES AIR MAIL GAME**   PARKER BROTHERS   1929
**THE AIR MAIL**   WOLVERINE   LITHO TIN   EARLY   1930s
**THE MAIL MUST FLY**   WHITMAN   1930s
**DC-3** (FROM A KIT)   STROMBECKER   WOOD   1930s

PARACHUTE JUMP GAME   MILTON BRADLEY CO.   1936

> This snub-winged plane keeps taking off but never gets off the ground.

"SUNNY ANDY" FLEET FLYER   WOLVERINE   18" LONG   1929

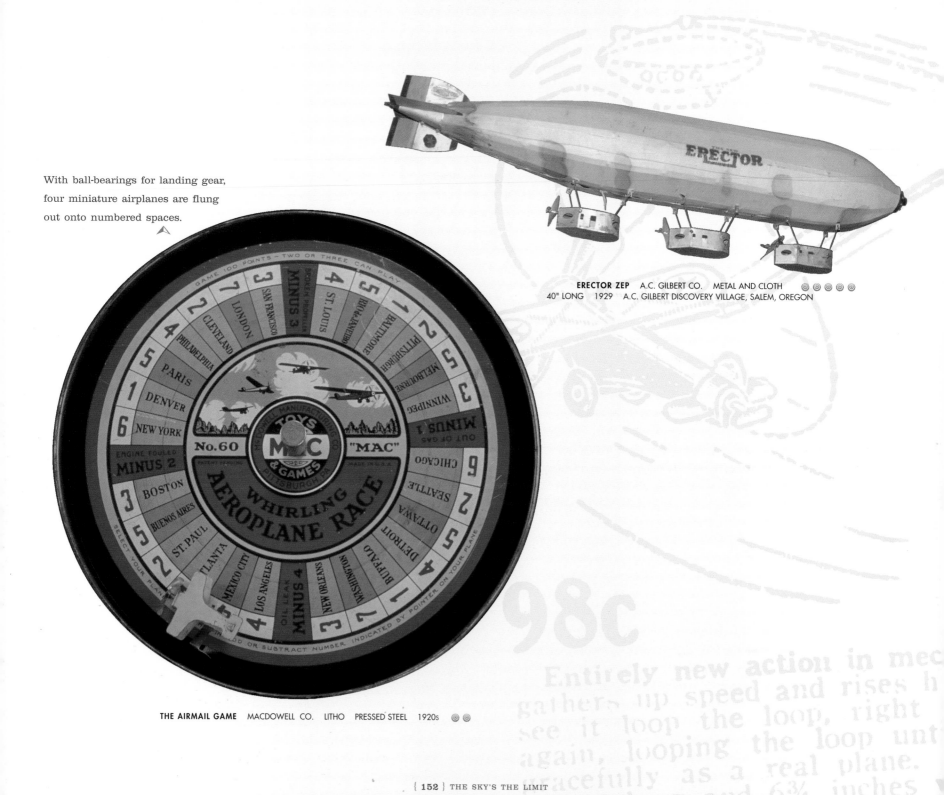

With ball-bearings for landing gear,
four miniature airplanes are flung
out onto numbered spaces.

**ERECTOR ZEP** A.C. GILBERT CO. METAL AND CLOTH ⊚ ⊚ ⊚ ⊚ ⊚
40" LONG 1929 A.C. GILBERT DISCOVERY VILLAGE, SALEM, OREGON

**THE AIRMAIL GAME** MACDOWELL CO. LITHO PRESSED STEEL 1920s ⊚ ⊚

98c

Entirely new action in mec
gathers up speed and rises h
see it loop the loop, right
again, looping the loop unt
gracefully as a real plane.
inches long and 6¾ inches
long. All parts made of m

"A true replica of the latest American Airlines
DC-4 Douglas 40 passenger sleeping plane."

AMERICAN AIRLINES DC-4   MARX   PRESSED STEEL   1940   26" WINGSPAN   $1.29   ◎ ◎ ◎

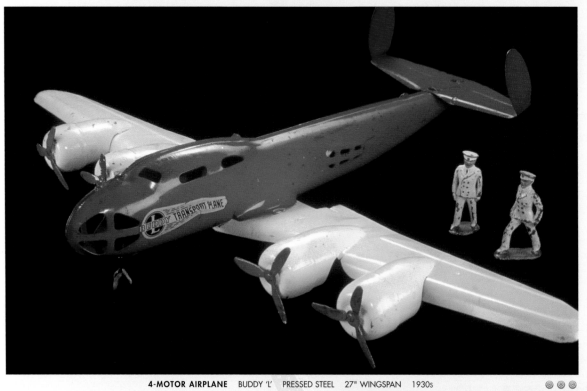

**4-MOTOR AIRPLANE**   BUDDY 'L'   PRESSED STEEL   27" WINGSPAN   1930s

**4-MOTOR AIRPLANE**   MARX   LITHO TIN
MECHANICAL   1938   18-1/2" WINGSPAN   $1.47

## 1936: Germany invades the Rhineland.

AVIATION TRAINING COCKPIT — COMPLETE COCKPIT AND COURSE IN HOW TO FLY   EINSEN-FREEMAN CORP., INC.   1942   $1

This is an extraordinary cardboard toy made at the beginning of the World War II featuring an authentic cockpit based on the Air Force Corp's Link Trainer. Includes wheel control, rudder pedals, a "Shoot Down Enemy Plane" spinner wheel, and booklets. All this for a dollar.

"Where else can we live but in the past? The future does not exist, that is truly the land of daydreams. The present flits by us second by second, not to be judged in its own terms...

# march of progress; the world expands

only as these ticks of the clock recede from us can we sort out the jumble of things into meaning..."

— GARY WILLS

MODERNITY WAS THE WATCHWORD of the 1920s and 1930s. The twenty-year span saw rising hemlines, streamlined trains, art deco skyscrapers, wireless radio sets, network radio programs, duplicating machines, plastic, surrealism, and on the silver screen the sophistication of Fred Astaire. Predominantly rural and insular, America had become decidedly urban and industrial, and despite the despair of the Depression, maintained an ongoing sense of progressive modernism.

In 1914 the Panama Canal had been completed. In 1919 Admiral Byrd had established Little America in the Antarctic. At the 1933 Chicago World's Fair, and again at the 1939 New York's World Fair (facilitated by the growth of media advertising and the appearance of credit which made buying easier), almost anything — despite the gathering storm in Europe — seemed possible.

Though the standard of living was much lower than today and individual opportunities for self-fulfillment were relatively limited, cooperation, teamwork, and an enforced civility was slowly bringing America out of the Depression. Combining old traditions with new discoveries in science, advances in technologies and the media, and with vehicles traveling over the land, sea, and through the air — all restyled to represent visions of the future, with travel itself representing a kind of modernity — America was pulling out of its insularity and opening itself to the world. It would be called "The American Century."

Smitty, the young office boy created by Walter Berndt, first appeared in 1922, immediately capturing an audience of millions. His determination to hit the big-time was the mood of America in the pre-Depression era.

**"SMITTY SCOOTER"**   MARX   LITHO TIN
MECHANICAL   8" HIGH   1922
**BOUND TO RISE**   HORATIO ALGER, JR.   THE WORLD PUBLISHING CO.   UNDATED

1937: Wilbur Shaw wins
his first of three Indianapolis 500 races.

**MARCH OF PROGRESS**   COLORING BOOK   ULLMAN MANUFACTURING CO.   1940   39¢

Four cardboard microphones are attached by string to playing pieces to be moved about "Little America," the Antarctic base established by Adm. Richard E. Byrd in 1928. Byrd was, disputably, the first to fly over the North Pole (1926) and, undisputedly, the South Pole (1929).

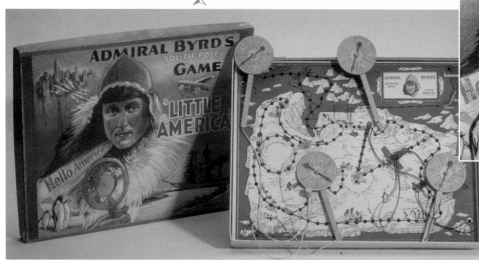

**ADMIRAL BYRD'S "LITTLE AMERICA" SOUTH POLE GAME**   PARKER BROTHERS INC.   1930   ◎ ◎ ◎ ◎

In the depth of the Depression, the 1933 Chicago World's Fair, like the New York World's Fair in 1939, emphasized a utopian vision of the future in which man, triumphing over nature, would enjoy a cleaner, safer, more harmonious world of tomorrow through labor saving devices — new machinery, new technologies — in factory and home. The result would be more leisure, entertainment, and creative time for everyone. An inspiring success, the Chicago World's Fair was held over into 1934. The Skyride over Lake Michigan was a principal attraction.

**CHICAGO WORLD'S FAIR SKYRIDE (ELECTRIC)**   PRESSED STEEL AND TIN
MANUFACTURER UNKNOWN   1933-34   EARL MILLER COLLECTION   ◎ ◎ ◎ ◎

COUPE WITH ELECTRIC LIGHTS   WYANDOTTE   PRESSED STEEL   7" LONG
LONESOME PINE HOUSE TRAILER   MARX   LITHO TIN   7" LONG
US 30 HIGHWAY SHIELD   ARCADE   3-1/2" HIGH

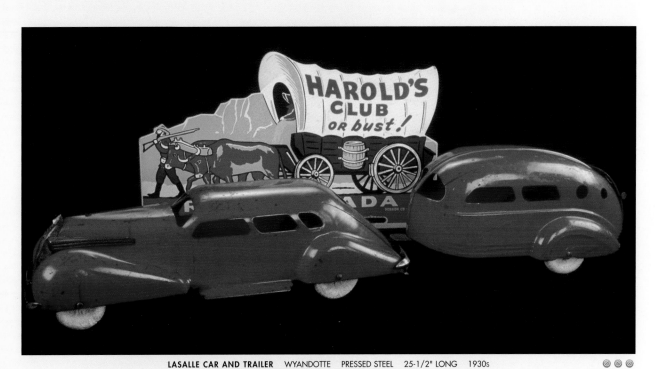

LASALLE CAR AND TRAILER   WYANDOTTE   PRESSED STEEL   25-1/2" LONG   1930s

"Increased trailers on the road have made children trailer minded so here is one with its spring driven coupe. They are both rubber tired and the trailer has orange curtains in each of its ten windows."

CHRYSLER AIR FLOW SEDAN (WITH LIGHTS) AND HOUSE TRAILER   KINGSBURY
PRESSED STEEL   MECHANICAL   DUDLEY MADDOX COLLECTION

While turning a crank, the driver tries to steer his car down an ever-changing roadway. If another car cuts you off, honk your horn. If you miss a curve — hmm, get out the Band-Aids.

A forerunner of today's video games.

1938: Germany invades Austria.

**TRAFFIC CONTROLLER W/RUBBER HORN**
MANUFACTURER UNKNOWN    PRESSED STEEL AND PAPER    c1949

**LINCOLN ZEPHYR SEDAN WITH BOAT AND TRAILER**
KINGSBURY    PRESSED STEEL    MECHANICAL    22-1/2" OVERALL    1937    $1.25

> Classical art deco styling. No other toy
> of the 1930s so exactly mirrors the
> architectural style of this period.

**GREYHOUND BUS TERMINAL**  MARX  LITHO TIN AND PRESSED STEEL  1930s

"Wind up this huge luxury liner of the highways and away she rolls."

GREYHOUND BUS (RESTORED)   KINGSBURY   PRESSED STEEL   18" LONG   MECHANICAL   1937
COWBOY (BOTTLE OPENER)   MANUFACTURER UNKNOWN   CAST IRON

"When wound the bus runs in a straight line or circle, stops automatically, the doors open, the bell rings and its stop lights are flashed. When the door closes the light goes off, the bell stops ringing and the bus travels on."

**GREYHOUND BUS**   BUDDY 'L'   MECHANICAL AND BATTERY   16" LONG   1940   $2.50   ⦿ ⦿ ⦿

"Go Greyhound and Leave the Driving to us."

**GREYHOUND BUS**   BUDDY 'L'   WOOD   18-1/4" LONG   1948
**MAN, WOMAN**   BARCLAY   LEAD   3-1/4" HIGH   1930s   ⦿ ⦿ ⦿

**INTERVAL PASSENGER BUS DELUXE**   KINGSBURY   PRESSED STEEL
MECHANICAL   1925   DUDLEY MADDOX COLLECTION

"Own Your Own Bus —
Just like the Interstate
motor buses you see on all
the country roadways..."

**ROYAL BUS LINE**   MARX   LITHO TIN   MECHANICAL   10" LONG   1926   48¢

**COACH**  BUDDY 'L'  PRESSED STEEL BODY WITH ALUMINUM DISC WHEELS  29-1/4" LONG  1927  BRAD CHAPMAN COLLECTION

Cars, trucks, and ambulances about the size of Cracker Jack prizes traverse a neo-Brooklyn Bridge — a wondrously charming reduction of the real world's busy bridges.

**BUSY BRIDGE**  MARX  LITHO TIN  MECHANICAL  1930  98¢

1938: Cincinnati Reds pitcher Johnny Vandermeer pitches two successive no-hit games.

**GEORGE WASHINGTON BRIDGE**   FRITZ BUESCHEL   LITHO TIN   MECHANICAL   21" LONG   1930s

LOWELL THOMAS' "WORLD CRUISE" GAME   PARKER BROTHERS   1937 ◎

Lowell Thomas was a
newscaster who was also
famous for his travelogues.

BALKY DONKEYS   MARX   1947   1930s   59¢
SOUTH OF THE BORDER   KENNEDY & CARR   1939
MEXICALI ROSE   STONE & TENNEY   1935

WORLD GLOBE   MANUFACTURER UNKNOWN   LITHO TIN   1934   23¢
PAN AMERICAN CHINA CLIPPER   WYANDOTTE   PRESSED STEEL   10-1/4" WINGSPAN   1937

listening to the radio;
a ticket to the movies

"...art is that in which
the hand, the head
and the heart of man
go together."

– JOHN RUSKIN

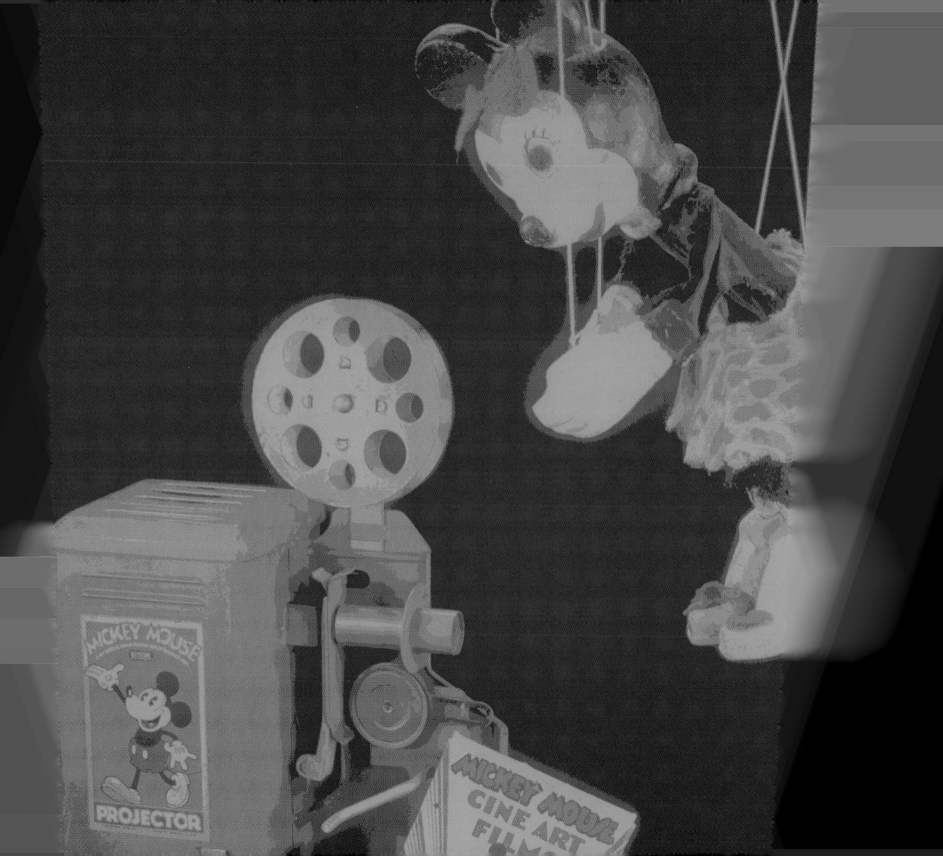

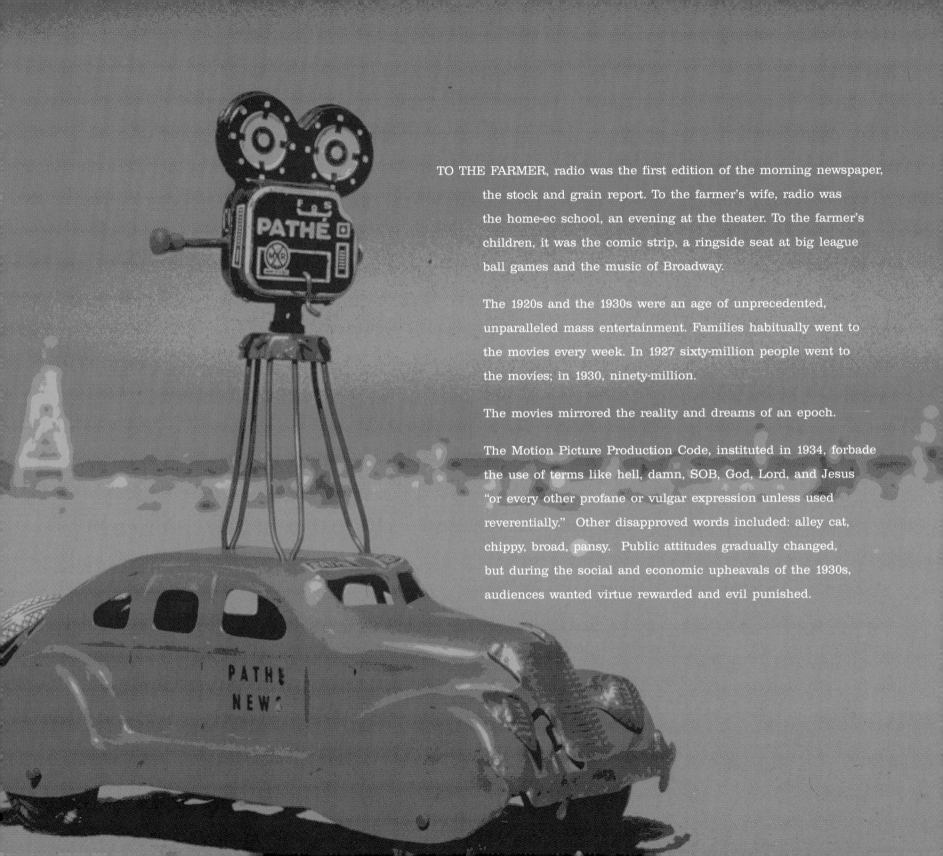

TO THE FARMER, radio was the first edition of the morning newspaper, the stock and grain report. To the farmer's wife, radio was the home-ec school, an evening at the theater. To the farmer's children, it was the comic strip, a ringside seat at big league ball games and the music of Broadway.

The 1920s and the 1930s were an age of unprecedented, unparalleled mass entertainment. Families habitually went to the movies every week. In 1927 sixty-million people went to the movies; in 1930, ninety-million.

The movies mirrored the reality and dreams of an epoch.

The Motion Picture Production Code, instituted in 1934, forbade the use of terms like hell, damn, SOB, God, Lord, and Jesus "or every other profane or vulgar expression unless used reverentially." Other disapproved words included: alley cat, chippy, broad, pansy. Public attitudes gradually changed, but during the social and economic upheavals of the 1930s, audiences wanted virtue rewarded and evil punished.

Wireless, or radio, developed in the 1920s from the possibility of transmitting and receiving sound at a distance. The invention meant that everyone could listen in real time, to all kinds of programs or information, anywhere.

**RADIO TINKER BANK**   THE TOY TINKERS   8-1/2" LONG   1922   $1
**LITTLE WONDER MICROPHONE**   WONDER SPECIALTIES CO.   1934

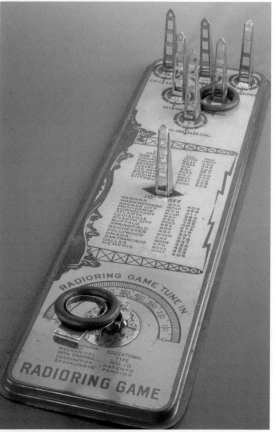

Place rubber ring
on metal holder
and shoot for your
transmitter mark!

**RADIO**   INTERPAPER GOODS CO.   1925        EACH:
**RADIO GAME**   MILTON BRADLEY CO.   1927

**RADIO RING GAME**
AMERICAN GAME & TOY CORP.   1926   89¢

**RADIO AMATEUR HOUR**
RADIO QUESTIONNAIRE CO. 1926
◉

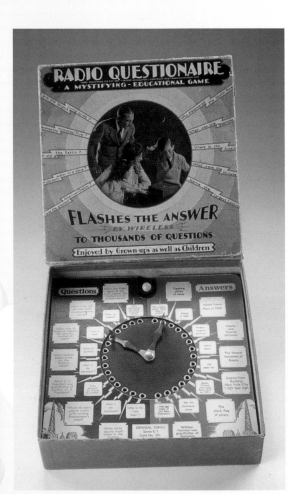

**RADIO QUESTIONNAIRE** RADIO QUESTIONNAIRE CO. ◉
BATTERY-OPERATED 1926 $1.48

Family evenings at home meant ◁
gathering around the radio to listen
to favorite programs.

**TOONIN RADIO GAME** ALL-FAIR 1925 79¢ ◉ ◉ ◉

The radio is white enamel on metal, the figure of Charlie a painted metal alloy.

"This comical car has spring-type bumpers, which, when hit, cause the car to reverse direction."

**CHARLIE MCCARTHY RADIO**   MAJESTIC RADIO CO.   1939
**CHARLIE MCCARTHY/MORTIMER SNERD "WE'LL MOW YOU DOWN" CAR**
MARX   LITHO TIN   MECHANICAL   15-1/2" LONG   1939

**AMOS 'N' ANDY WALKERS**   MARX   TIN LITHO
MECHANICAL   11" HIGH   1930   89¢ EACH; $1.34 A PAIR

Amos 'n' Andy, written and performed by two small-time, white vaudeville performers, Freeman Gosden and Charles Correll, debuted on Chicago's WMAQ on March 19, 1928. On August 19, 1929, it premiered nationally on NBC. By 1931, the program had become a national legend, with an estimated one-third of Americans tuning in. Even movie theatres timed their showings to allow a fifteen-minute break so the episode could be piped in.

**CHARLIE McCARTHY'S BENZINE BUGGY**   MARX   LITHO TIN   MECHANICAL   7-1/8" LONG   1938   49¢
**MORTIMER SNERD CAR**   MARX   LITHO TIN   MECHANICAL   7-1/8" LONG   1939   49¢

The Edgar Bergen and Charlie McCarthy Show first aired in 1937 and continued through the 1940s as a weekly prime-time radio comedy show. The original Charlie McCarthy dummy is on display at the Smithsonian Institution's National Museum of American History in Washington, D.C.

**CHARLIE McCARTHY**   EFFANBEE   20" HIGH   LATE 1930s
**CHARLIE McCARTHY**   MANUFACTURER UNKNOWN
(COMPOSITION)   13" HIGH   LATE 1930s

This is not a "legitimate" toy but one that, finding a legless Charlie at a flea market, a collector enthusiast made up. The pressed steel Jeep was made by Marx in 1947.

**CHARLIE McCARTHY DRIVES A JEEP**

PUFFED WHEAT — BABE RUTH PREMIUMS ADVERTISEMENT

"Return with us now to those thrilling days of yesteryear when..."
(When a cereal box top and a dime brought in the mail wonderful,
wonderful things — shakeup mugs and badges and decoders,
telescopes, Hike-o-Meters, and secret whistle rings...)

RADIO PREMIUM PINS: BUCK JONES CLUB HORSESHOE PIN          EACH: ◉
MELVIN PURVIS JR. G-MAN BADGE
DICK TRACY BADGE

Bigger than life, the radio serial
programs were united in the basic
principles of right and wrong.
There was always treachery of
some sort, or mystery, and it was
easy to feel a part of the action,
because all the activity took place
in your mind's eye.

WHEATIES' JACK ARMSTRONG PREMIUMS ADVERTISEMENT

WHEATIES BOX, SHOOTING PROPELLOR PLANE GUN, HIKE-O-METER,
BULLET FLASHLIGHT, EXPLORER TELESCOPE, CEREAL BOWL,
JACK ARMSTRONG AND THE IVORY TREASURE BIG LITTLE BOOK

In 1935-36, 300,000 kids sent in Wheaties box tops to receive "Jack Armstrong's latest invention," Daisy Mfg. Company's "Propellor Plane Gun" that shot a spinning disk into the air.

1939: Germany invades Poland;
the Draft is instituted in the U.S.

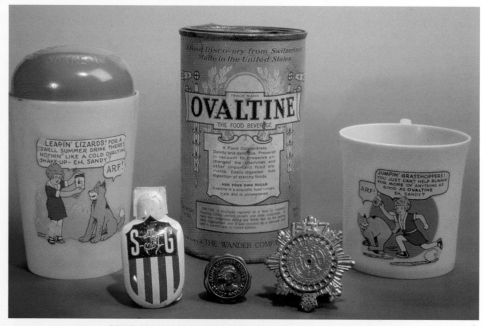

RADIO ORPHAN ANNIE PREMIUMS WITH SPONSOR'S OVALTINE CAN:
SHAKEUP MUG, SIGNAL CLICKER, SECRET SOCIETY PIN, DECODER, BEETLEWARE MUG

ORPHAN ANNIE CIRCUS CUT-OUTS (PREMIUM)   CARDBOARD   1936   ◉ ◉

SHIRLEY TEMPLE PREMIUMS: BLUE DEPRESSION GLASS MUG, BOWL, AND PITCHER (HONEYCOMB PATTERN BY HAZEL ATLAS GLASS CO. MADE FOR DISTRIBUTION AS A FREE PREMIUM FOR GOLD MEDAL FOODS, 1935).

A Kellogg's Rice Krispies Cereal Premium. The premium's recipient cut three dolls from printed cloth, then sewed and stuffed them. ◢

SNAP! CRACKLE! AND POP! DOLLS    MANUFACTURER UNKNOWN    CLOTH    14-1/2" HIGH    1930s

**BETTY BOOP** COMPOSITION HEAD
ON AN ARTICULATED WOOD BODY
MADE BY JOSEPH KALLUS 12-1/2" HIGH
PAUL AND KATIE HEDBURN COLLECTION
⦾ ⦾ ⦾ ⦾ ⦾

Betty Boop, the ageless vamp, the "Boop-Oop-a-Doop"
flapper holdout from the 1920s Jazz Age, made her first
appearance in Max Fleisher's Talkathon in 1930.

**THE MOVING PICTURE GAME** MILTON BRADLEY CO. 1929 ⦾ ⦾

**MOVIE-LAND KEENO** WILDER MFG. CO. 1929 ⦾

**HAROLD LLOYD BELL RINGER** (PLUNGER ACTION)
NIFTY   LITHO TIN   6-1/2" HIGH   1920s

**JUVENILE MOVIE MAKEUP KIT**   MINERS, INC.   1937

"Put on a double feature for your friends! Film is fed into the light evenly. Nickel-plated rollers hold film against the sprocket. Other features: self-framing device to bring film into perfect alignment, fine quality clear-focus lens, jointed stand to throw pictures at any vertical angle, and a reel large enough to hold 100 ft. of film. Simple to thread — a child can operate it. Ventilated lamp house prevents over heating."

The projector was hand-cranked using an ordinary electric light bulb.

**KOMIC KAMERA VIEWER, FRANK BUCK, MUTT & JEFF, MOVIE KOMICS VIEWER**
OTHER 16MM. FILMS: —
TOM MIX, AMOS 'N' ANDY, JUS FELLAS, COMIC FILMS
HAPPY HOOLIGAN, BETTY BOOP, KRAZY KAT, POPEYE
MICKEY MOUSE, BARNEY GOOGLE, OUR GANG, CHARLIE CHAPLIN
W. C. FIELDS, WILLIAM S. HART, WOODY WOODPECKER, ABBOTT & COSTELLO

**MICKEY MOUSE 16MM MOVIE PROJECTOR**
KEYSTONE MANUFACTURING CO.    LITHO TIN    10-1/2" HIGH    1935    $4.85
**MICKEY MOUSE 16MM FILM**    CINE ART    1935    50 FT.    $1.59
25" 16MM POPEYE 87¢; MICKEY MOUSE 63¢
**MINNIE MOUSE MARIONETTE**    GUND TOY CO.    10" HIGH    1930

Pathé and Movietone cameramen covered the world, providing weekly three- to five-minute news highlights to theater chains. Stalwart cameramen were regularly seen at major events, often elevated above the crowd on a platform mounted atop their car.

**PATHÉ NEWS CAR** (LINCOLN ZEPHYR STYLING) **WITH CAMERA**   MARX   PRESSED STEEL   10" LONG (CAMERA 6" HIGH)   1936   49¢   ⊚ ⊚ ⊚ ⊚ ⊚

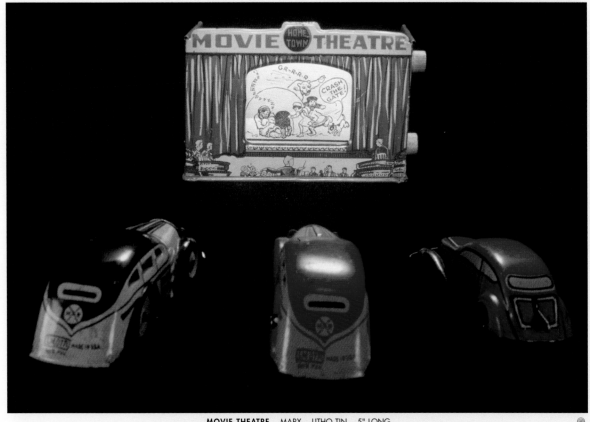

**MOVIE THEATRE**   MARX   LITHO TIN   5" LONG
**TRICKY TAXI**   MARX   LITHO TIN   MECHANICAL   4-1/2" LONG   1935   25¢
**SEDAN**   MARX   LITHO TIN   MECHANICAL   4-1/2" LONG   1936   25¢

After the war, Americans by the millions went to drive-in movie theaters. A main attraction of drive-ins was that the whole family could pile into the car and see a movie with all the comforts of home — blankets, pillows, snacks, and privacy. No babysitter needed. And if you were a teenager on a date — well.

"The concept of beauty is that which is admirable, which pleases upon being seen."

— MORTIMER ADLER

# theatrical world; the sound of — music?

"In life beauty perishes, but not in a good toy."

— GERRIT BEVERWYCK

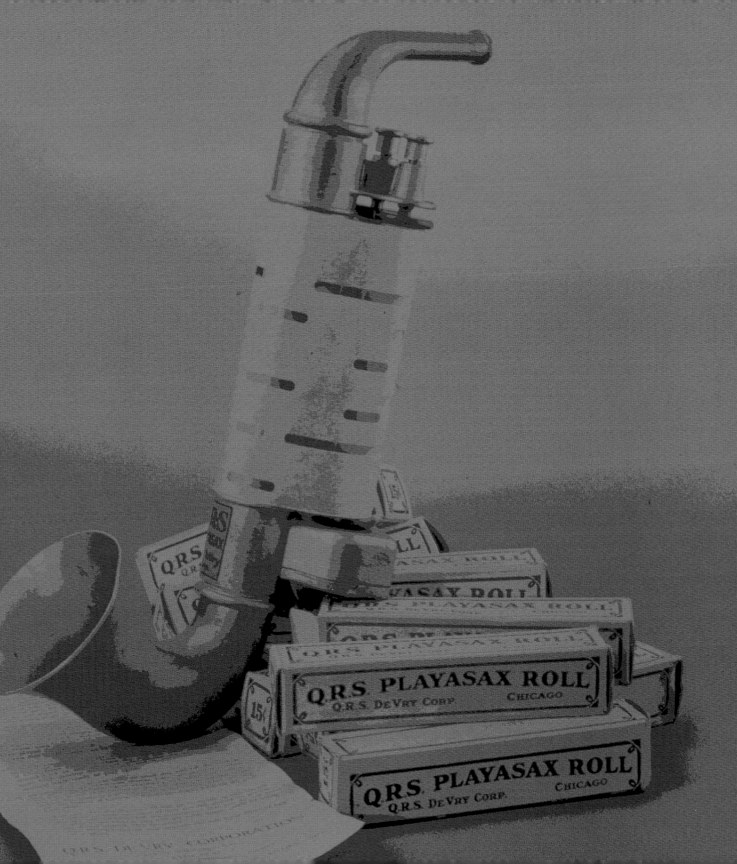

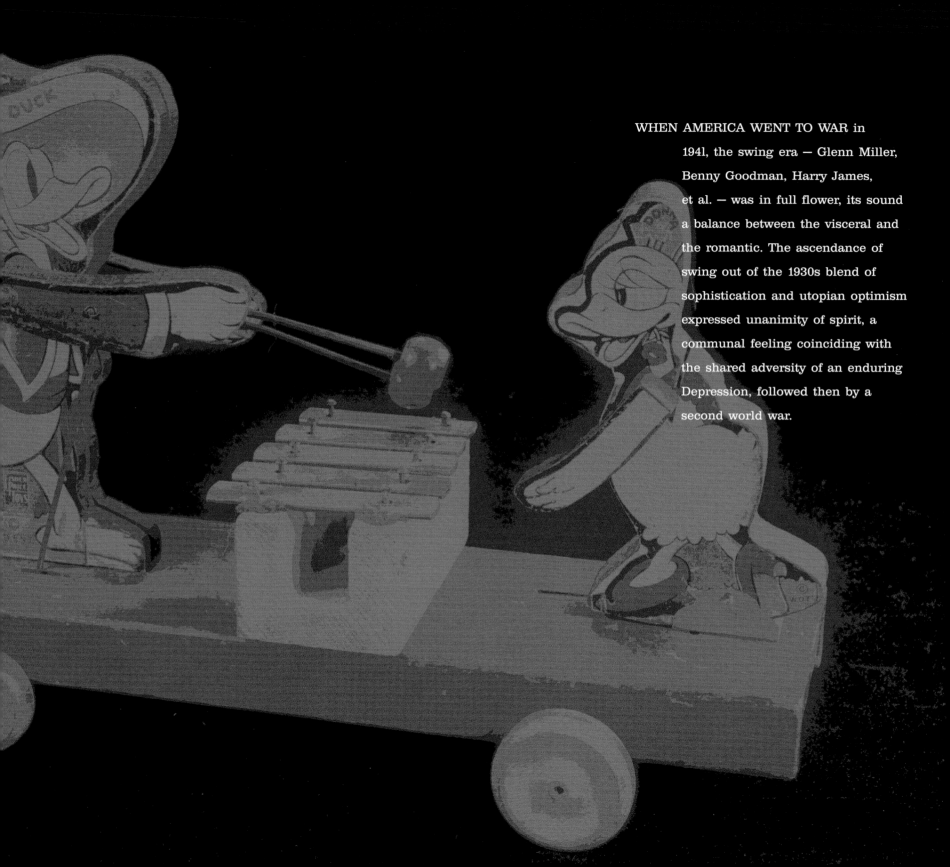

WHEN AMERICA WENT TO WAR in 1941, the swing era — Glenn Miller, Benny Goodman, Harry James, et al. — was in full flower, its sound a balance between the visceral and the romantic. The ascendance of swing out of the 1930s blend of sophistication and utopian optimism expressed unanimity of spirit, a communal feeling coinciding with the shared adversity of an enduring Depression, followed then by a second world war.

THIMBLE THEATRE MYSTERY PLAYHOUSE   HARDING PRODUCTS   1939 ●●●◉

Composition figures Popeye, Olive Oyl, and Whimpy can be moved about this Thimble Theatre in any manner the child-director wishes.

A rare, heavy cardboard lithographed Punch and Judy ring toss toy.

PUNCH AND JUDY   AMERICAN TOY WORKS   1930 ●●

"It's difficult for youngsters to recognize each other when one suddenly grows a beard, a red nose, large floppy ears, etc., but it's very amusing and always brings a hearty laugh...set includes facial parts — nose, ears, hair for beard, side burns, whiskers, etc. A monocle for special occasions."

DELUXE DISGUISE KIT   F.A.O. SCHWARTZ   1940s   $2.50 ●

**ASK ME ANOTHER**
MARX   CARDBOARD W/BATTERY   1926   94¢

**MYSTIC WRITING**   WILDER MFG. CO.   1920s

**MIRACULUM GAME**   MANUFACTURER UNKNOWN   1920s

"Tricks for the pocket or stage. Simple and easy to perform, including the famous and mysterious Photoplasmic Mystery, Cut and Restore Paper Ribbon, Multiplying Cars, Multiplying Coins, Vanishing Handkerchief, Buddha Money Mystery, Phantom Card Trick, Galloping Dime, Hiding Chessman, Spiral Wire Illusion."

**MAGIC SET**   A.C. GILBERT   1930   95¢

**GILBERT HANDKERCHIEF TRICKS**   A.C. GILBERT CO.   JOHN DRURY COLLECTION

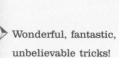

Wonderful, fantastic, unbelievable tricks!

1941: Ted Williams hits .406 for the season; Joe DiMaggio hits safely in 56 consecutive games.

A saw-toothed bar pulled through the base of the ballerina's skirt causes her to spin like a top.

**BALLERINA** MARX LITHO TIN
GYROSCOPIC ACTION 5-1/2" HIGH 29¢

**BANJO PLAYER** (JAZZBO JIM)
MARX LITHO TIN MECHANICAL

**VIOLIN PLAYER** (SPIC AND SPAN)
MARX LITHO TIN MECHANICAL

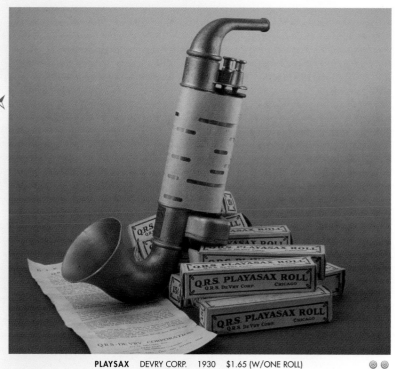

Cranking a
perforated paper
roll allows young
musicians to
quickly and easily
play — music?

**PLAYSAX**   DEVRY CORP.   1930   $1.65 (W/ONE ROLL)

**DRUMMER** (SPIC AND SPAN)
MARX   LITHO TIN   MECHANICAL

Humorist Bob Burns's
"Bazooka," because of its
similar shape, inspired the
name for a new weapon
the U.S. Army adopted in
the second World War.

**BOB BURNS "BAZOOKA"**   M. POCHAPIN, INC.   1938

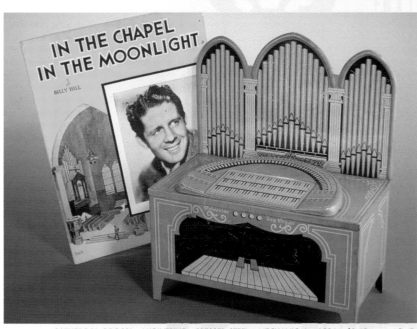

CATHEDRAL ORGAN  WOLVERINE  PRESSED STEEL  MECHANICAL  1936  $1.65
IN THE CHAPEL IN THE MOONLIGHT  BILLY HILL

"Musicians marvel at the remarkable
performance of this new play organ
with its rich, full-bodied Cathedral tones.
By turning the crank at the rear, the
organ renders bar after bar of inspiring
harmonies. Player can make the tone
loud or soft by speeding up or slowing
down the turning of the crank."

"These pianos are made by craftsmen who
have the reputation for building the finest
of all toy pianos. Accurately tuned, finished
in shiny rosewood color. Keys made of
wood, painted with black markings to
imitate flats and sharps. Simple melodies
can be played by the little miss. A book of
instructions furnished with each piano.
Six sizes to choose from."

PIANO  SCHOENHUT  WOOD  1920  7 KEY TO 22 KEY: $1 TO $4.59
PAUL AND KATIE HEDBURN COLLECTION

"Just Think. A Mouse orchestra. Surely a merry gang. Watch the little fellow on the piano direct the show and the fellow on the side drumming away while another one sits at the piano and the fourth one jigs showing us some clever dancing steps."

Art Deco styling. The deluxe version of this toy came with a marquee and a violinist sitting atop the piano. Another version is without the marquee and instead of a violinist, a band director. The Merry Makers are an obvious take-off on Mickey Mouse. Louis Marx chose not to obtain a license from Disney for this toy and instead contrived his own mouse — mice.

**MARX MERRY MAKERS**   MARX   LITHO TIN   MECHANICAL   1929   98¢   ◎ ◎ ◎ ◎ ◎

For nearly forty years, the satirical genius Al Capp drew the "Li'l Abner" comic strip (Pappy, Mammy, Daisy Mae, the Shmoo, Clark Bagel, Henry Cabbage Cod, Kickapoo Joy Juice). His characters can be read on two levels — as country bumpkins, or as satirical views of American society.

**LI'L ABNER BAND**   UNIQUE ART MFG. CO.   LITHO TIN   MECHANICAL   1945   ⊚ ⊚ ⊚ ⊚

"When you plink out a tune, Mickey and Minnie dance gaily above the keyboard."

**MICKEY MOUSE PIANO**
MARKS BROTHERS   WOOD   1935   10" LONG   $1   ⊚ ⊚ ⊚ ⊚

Came with (3) 3" metal records: "Sidewalks of New York," "My Old Kentucky Home," and "Farmer in the Dell."

Other records available: "My Bonnie Lies Over the Ocean" "Wearing of the Green" "Good Night, Ladies" "Silent Night" "Yankee Doodle" "The Mocking Bird"

**ZILOTONE**   WOLVERINE   PRESSED STEEL   MECHANICAL   ⊚ ⊚ ⊚
(WHEN WOUND, A 5-INCH CLOWN FIGURE TURNS ON PLATFORM WITH HAMMER)
1929   $2.50

**MICKEY MOUSE BAND** FISHER-PRICE LITHO PAPER ON WOOD 1935 89¢ EACH: ◎ ◎ ◎
**MICKEY MOUSE XYLOPHONE** FISHER-PRICE LITHO PAPER ON WOOD/METAL 1939

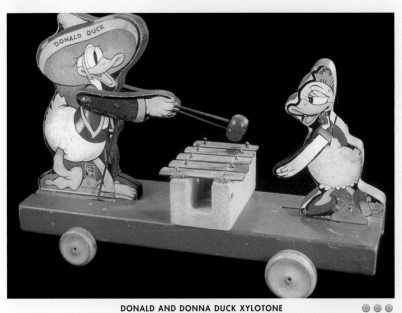

**DONALD AND DONNA DUCK XYLOTONE**
FISHER-PRICE LITHO PAPER ON WOOD/METAL 11" LONG 1937 98¢ ◎ ◎ ◎

**DONALD DUCK BANDLEADER** KNICKERBOCKER TOY CO. CLOTH
19" HIGH 1938 PAUL AND KATIE HEDBURN COLLECTION ◎ ◎ ◎ ◎ ◎

**TEDDY BEAR PARADE**   FISHER-PRICE   LITHO PAPER ON WOOD   1938   ◎ ◎ ◎

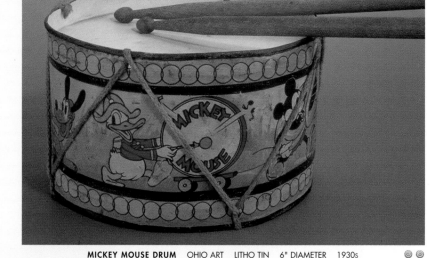

**MICKEY MOUSE DRUM**   OHIO ART   LITHO TIN   6" DIAMETER   1930s   ◎ ◎

**DOC AND DOPEY DWARFS**   FISHER-PRICE   LITHO PAPER ON WOOD   1938   ◎ ◎ ◎ ◎

➤This beautifully lithographed Doc and Dopey pull toy (it does make a clatter) was produced in Fisher-Price's seventh year of production. It and the other superior Fisher-Price toys produced in the company's first years (founded in 1931 at the height of the Depression) perhaps accounts for how the company survived and continued to prosper.

Popeye dances a sailor's hornpipe as Olive swings and sways to the sounds of her accordion...

**POPEYE AND OLIVE OYL ON ROOF**   MARX   LITHO TIN   MECHANICAL   1930

"Art is a higher
type of knowledge
than experience."

– ARISTOTLE

# the comics

"I know it's art
when it makes
the back of
my neck prickle."

– JANE STEDMAN

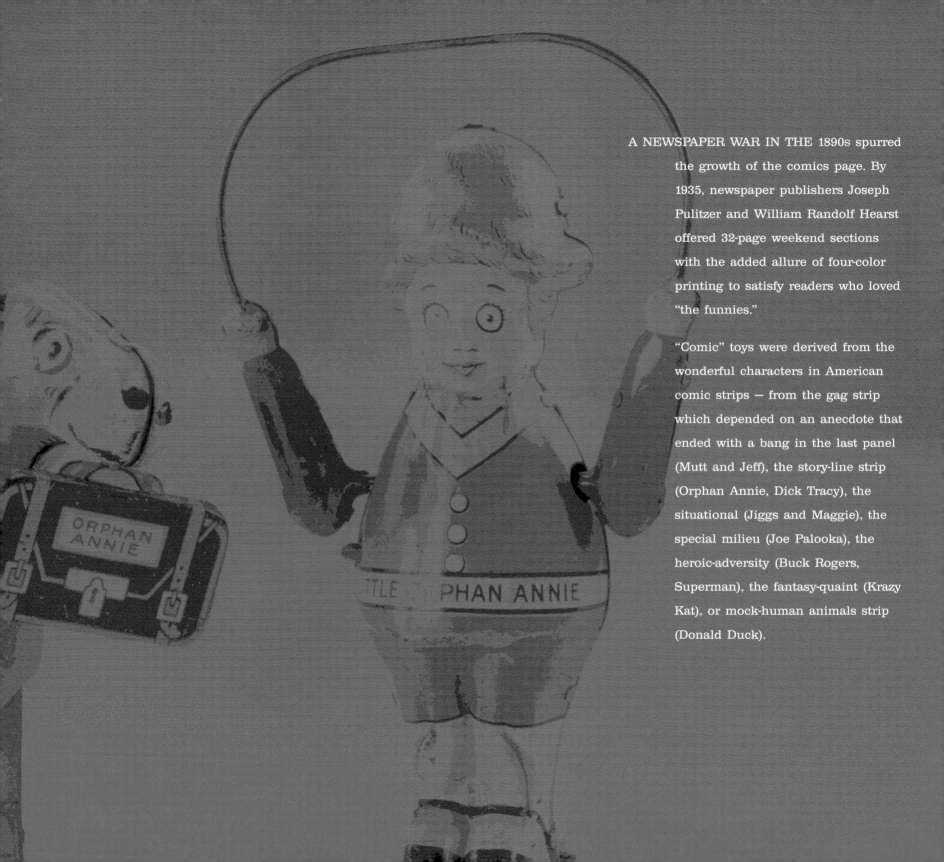

A NEWSPAPER WAR IN THE 1890s spurred the growth of the comics page. By 1935, newspaper publishers Joseph Pulitzer and William Randolf Hearst offered 32-page weekend sections with the added allure of four-color printing to satisfy readers who loved "the funnies."

"Comic" toys were derived from the wonderful characters in American comic strips — from the gag strip which depended on an anecdote that ended with a bang in the last panel (Mutt and Jeff), the story-line strip (Orphan Annie, Dick Tracy), the situational (Jiggs and Maggie), the special milieu (Joe Palooka), the heroic-adversity (Buck Rogers, Superman), the fantasy-quaint (Krazy Kat), or mock-human animals strip (Donald Duck).

**OFFICER 666** MARX LITHO TIN MECHANICAL 1931 48¢ EACH: ◎ ◎ ◎ ◎
**MAMMY'S BOY** (A TAKE-OFF ON COMEDIAN EDDIE CANTOR?)
MARX LITHO TIN MECHANICAL 1929 57¢
**FUNNY FACE** (A TAKE-OFF ON COMEDIAN HAROLD LLOYD?) MARX LITHO TIN MECHANICAL 1928 65¢
**AMOS** MARX LITHO TIN MECHANICAL 1929 57¢
**ANDY** MARX LITHO TIN MECHANICAL 1929 57¢

Amos Jones and Andrew Brown came on the national scene March 19, 1928, courtesy of Charles Correll and Freeman Gosden, and soon became the most popular program in radio history. Amos was simple, trusting, unsophisticated; Andy, lazy, domineering, always browbeating Amos, but always protecting his friend from others' jokes.

These remarkable litho tin mechanical "walkers" with their shuffling gaits and changing facial expressions ("Watch them roll their eyes as they shuffle along on their big feet") stand 11 inches high.

1943: Lyricist Richard Rodgers and composer Oscar Hammerstein's *Oklahoma!* premieres on Broadway.

"A rolling ball target game...."

**FUNNY POPS** ALLIED MFG. CO. CARDBOARD 12" X 14" 1936 ◎ ◎

"When mechanism is wound, Orphan Annie skips rope. If she falls she gets up herself to an upright position, never stopping her rope jumping, regardless of whether she falls on her back or on her face. This toy is just as full of pep and action as the Orphan Annie you see in the comics."

Cartoonist Harold Gray's tough little orphan with her reddish orange hair and a heart of gold survived as a comic strip for more than fifty years, only occasionally needing the help of protector Daddy Warbucks when events became too precarious. Her first appearance was in 1924.

**SANDY** (STARTLINGLY INTELLIGENT DOG)   MARX   LITHO TIN
MECHANICAL   1931   25¢

**LITTLE ORPHAN ANNIE**   MARX LITHO TIN   MECHANICAL   1931   25¢

**LITTLE ORPHAN ANNIE DOLL**
LONG LIVE TOY CO.   OIL CLOTH   1927
PAUL AND KATIE HEDBURN COLLECTION

**BARNEY GOOGLE GAME**   MILTON BRADLEY   1923   79¢
**BARNEY GOOGLE RIDING SPARK PLUG**   NIFTY   LITHO TIN
MECHANICAL   7-1/2" LONG   1924

When wound, Spark Plug moves forward, Barney jumps up and down as Spark Plug's head and tail flits up and down. The Billy DeBeck cartoon, debuting in 1916, featuring saucer-eyed Barney and his pal was a favorite through the 1920s and into the 1930s. Though disaster prone, Barney's cheerful belief that he could someday straighten everything out endeared him to millions of readers.

Rudy, an ostrich, was a
most troublesome friend
of Barney Google.

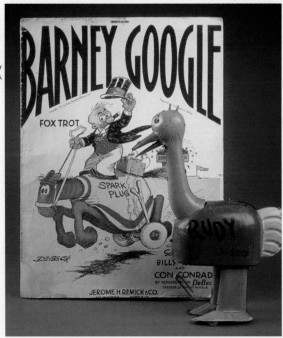

**RUDY**   NIFTY   LITHO TIN (BODY ONLY,
THE REMAINDER HAND-PAINTED)   MECHANICAL   9" HIGH   1924
**MUSIC SHEET BARNEY GOOGLE**   JEROME H. REMICK

**KAYO DOLL**   11-1/2" TALL   COMPOSITION
FAMOUS ARTISTS SYNDICATE

**MOON MULLINS GAME**   MILTON BRADLEY   20¢
**MOON (MOONSHINE) MULLINS HANDCAR**   MARX   PRESSED STEEL   MECHANICAL   6" LONG   1934

**SMITTY GAME** MILTON BRADLEY EARLY 1930s 20¢

1944: D-Day –
   the Allies invade Europe.
GI Bill of Rights is signed.

"The Little King" was created in the early 1930s
by Otto Soglow. This toy, made of painted wood,
"walks" when a string is pulled in the Little King's
crown, activating a rubber-band tensioned axle.

**LITTLE KING** JAYMAR WOOD 4" HIGH 1940s 25¢

"Snowflakes and Swipes," a short-lived comic strip by Oscar Hitt, the creator of Highway Henry, portrayed the adventures of a small African-American boy and his dog, Swipes, who was always a vexation.

**SNOWFLAKES AND SWIPES**   NIFTY   7-1/2" LONG   1929   25¢   PAUL AND KATIE HEDBURN COLLECTION

A clockwork mechanism at one end of the toy makes ◄
the toy stop and start and go backward and forward.
The two ends of the toy are connected by a thin
two-inch strip of spring steel that forces the figures to
jump back and forth at each other. George McManus's
"Bringing Up Father" comic strip, starring Maggie and
Jiggs, survived for more than sixty years.

**MAGGIE AND JIGGS**   NIFTY   LITHO TIN   MECHANICAL   7" LONG   1924   ◉ ◉ ◉ ◉ ◉

**PUZZLES: JUST KIDS; KATZENJAMMERS, ANDY GUMP, LITTLE ORPHAN ANNIE**   WHITMAN   1930s   ◉ ◉

Sidney Smith's "The Gumps," starring Andy Gump, a tall chin-less, wispy-haired man, his wife Min and son Chester was the most popular comic strip of its day. Featuring Andy's ridiculously proportioned clunker car with its huge disc wheels, the strip made the auto a joy to behold — just looking at it and its driver made you laugh. Depression era hard times befell the Andy Gump car, and in 1931 it was discontinued.

**ANDY GUMP GAME**   MILTON BRADLEY   1924   20¢
**ANDY GUMP 348 CAR**
ARCADE   CAST IRON   1923-1931   7-1/8" LONG

"Action pull toy with jointed legs and feet mounted on pedals of cycle which go up and down when toy is pulled along. Each time the gear wheel is turned Ignatz squeaks."

The bane of George
Herriman's Krazy Kat,
Ignatz was just a wee mouse.
Some mouse!

**SQUEAKING IGNATZ**   CHEIN   WOOD   9" HIGH   1932   $1

**JIMINY CRICKET DOLL** KNICKERBOCKER DOLL CO. ◎ ◎ ◎

Of all the comic Kickerbocker dolls, Jiminy Cricket, Pinocchio's companion in the Disney film, is surely one of the most delightful.

1945: President Roosevelt dies.
Vice-president Harry Truman becomes President.
Germany surrenders.
The United Nations is established.

Henry, a comic strip character created by Carl Anderson, is hairless, expressionless, and speechless. Because there is no text, the comic strip relied entirely on the gag.

**HENRY** SUN RUBBER 1940
**EASTMAN KODAK "BROWNIE" BOX CAMERA** 1900

...The U.S. drops atomic bombs on Hiroshima and Nagasaki, Japan. Japan surrenders.

**UNCLE WIGGILY'S HOLLOW STUMP BUNGALOW**   PRESSED CARDBOARD
MANUFACTURER UNKNOWN   1920s   ◎ ◎ ◎

This old house was a promotional display.
In good weather it stands 11 inches high;
in bad weather, not quite.

Popeye the ◁
Sailor, star of The
Thimble Theatre,
was created in 1929
by Elsie Segar.

**POPEYE MENU BAGATELLE**   ◎ ◎ ◎
DURABLE TOY AND NOVELTY CO.   1935

"Wind up Popeye ◁
and he walks in his
queer sailor stride,
carrying his parrots."

**POPEYE WITH PARROT CAGES**   ◎ ◎ ◎
MARX   LITHO TIN   MECHANICAL   8-1/4" HIGH   1935   25¢
**POPEYE**   (COMPOSITION)   KING FEATURES SYNDICATE   1935   ◎ ◎ ◎
**POPEYE EXPRESS**   MARX   LITHO TIN   MECHANICAL   1935   25¢   ◎ ◎ ◎

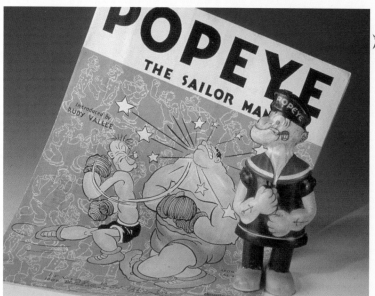

POPEYE served as an example to children to eat nutritious vegetables — particularly spinach, from which he gained his enormous strength.

**POPEYE WALKER**  CHEIN  LITHO TIN  MECHANICAL  6-1/4"  1930s
**"POPEYE THE SAILOR MAN" SHEET MUSIC**  INTRODUCED BY RUDY VALLEE

**POPEYE RING TOSS TARGET**  JOSEPH SCHNEIDER CO.  LITHO TIN  1930s

**POPEYE MENU TARGET**
DURABLE TOY AND NOVELTY CO.  1935

**JEEP**  COMPOSITION  CAMEO DOLL CO.  1936
**POPEYE PLAYING CARD GAME**  WHITMAN  1936
**"POPEYE SEES THE SEA"**  BIG LITTLE BOOK  1936

**POPPIN' POPEYE**  JOSEPH SCHNEIDER INC.  1930s

"Felix the Cat" was a Pat Sullivan comic strip distributed by King Features.
It originated as an animated movie cartoon in 1920.

"When pulled along floor Felix squeaks and moves up and down with a comical expression."

**SPEEDY FELIX** NIFTY MANUFACTURER UNKNOWN PAINTED WOOD W/LEATHERETTE EARS 11-3/4" LONG 1925 89¢ ◎◎◎◎
**FELIX DOLL** MANUFACTURER UNKNOWN COMPOSITION 1930s ◎◎◎◎
**FELIX** SCHOENHUT WOOD AND LEATHER 1940 ◎◎◎◎

"Imagine Felix not being ◁ able to catch the two mice he is chasing. That's just what happens on this snappy action toy. Felix chases them harder than ever as this all-metal toy is pulled along but he never quite catches up."

**FELIX CHASES MICE**   NIFTY   LITHO TIN   7-1/2" LONG   25¢   ◎ ◎ ◎

**MICKEY MOUSE HOOP-LA**   MARKS BROS.   1930s   ◎ ◎

**MICKEY MOUSE PULL TOY**
N.N. HILL BRASS CO.   LITHO PAPER ON WOOD AND PRESSED STEEL   13" LONG   c1935   ◎ ◎ ◎

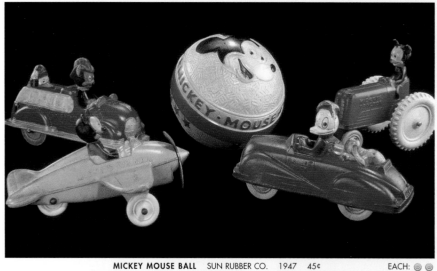

"You can almost see how fast the Fire truck and Roadster are going as Donald holds his hat and Pluto clings to the rumble seat..."

**MICKEY MOUSE BALL**  SUN RUBBER CO.  1947  45¢  EACH: ◎ ◎
**MICKEY MOUSE FIREMAN**  SUN RUBBER CO.  6" LONG  1938  65¢
**MICKEY MOUSE TRACTOR**  SUN RUBBER CO.  6" LONG  1938  65¢
**MICKEY MOUSE AIRPLANE**  SUN RUBBER CO.  6" LONG  1938  65¢
**DONALD DUCK COUPE**  SUN RUBBER CO.  6" LONG  1938  65¢

Their mechanisms derived from army surplus, 11,000 watches were sold on Macy's first day of sale.

**MICKEY MOUSE WRISTWATCH**
INGERSOLL-WATERBURY WATCH CO.  1933  $2.95  ◎ ◎ ◎

"Carefully constructed.  Made to spin by pressing plunger up and down. Actually plays four chords."

**MICKEY MOUSE TOP**  OHIO ART  LITHO TIN  9" DIAMETER  1939  47¢  ◎ ◎ ◎

A bagatelle, ◀
or "pinball" game.

**MICKEY MOUSE BAGATELLE** MARKS BROTHERS
LITHO PAPER ON WOOD 1934

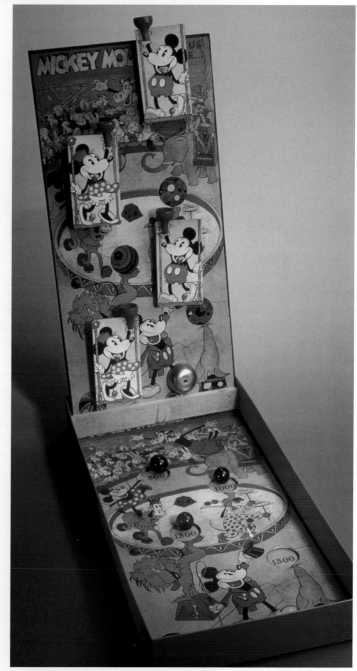

**MICKEY MOUSE COMING HOME GAME** MARKS BROTHERS 1930s ◎◎◎

SNOW WHITE CARNIVAL CHALK DOLL   1930s-1950s
SNOW WHITE SAND PAIL   OHIO ART   1938
SNOW WHITE PUZZLE   MARX   1939

"Whistle While You Work" sheet music
Larry Morey and Frank Churchill

Of all the Snow White and Seven Dwarfs
dolls produced after the enormous success of
Disney's groundbreaking animated film, these
Knickerbocker likenesses have the greatest
charm of all.

THE SEVEN DWARFS   KNICKERBOCKER DOLL CO.   COMPOSITION   ARTICULATED   9" HIGH   1939

**SNOW WHITE** ◎ ◎ ◎ ◎ ◎
KNICKERBOCKER DOLL CO.   COMPOSITION   ARTICULATED
12-1/2" HIGH   1938   PAUL AND KATIE HEDBURN COLLECTION

Superman, the last survivor from the far off planet Krypton, attempts to stop and turn over an evil-looking pilot's airplane (he almost always succeeds). Superman was created by Jerry Siegel and Joe Shuster in 1933, both of whom were seventeen years old — teenagers.

**SUPERMAN AIRPLANE**   MARX   LITHO TIN   MECHANICAL   6-1/2" LONG   1940   CHUCK MARANTO COLLECTION ◎ ◎ ◎ ◎ ◎

1946: Churchill delivers
"Iron Curtain" speech

THE ADVENTURES OF BUCK ROGERS   WHITMAN   1934          EACH: ◉
BUCK ROGERS PENCIL BOX   AMERICAN LEAD PENCIL CO   1936
BUCK ROGERS BIG LITTLE BOOK   WHITMAN   1934

BUCK ROGERS ROCKET SHIP BOX

➤An example of some of
the excellent toy-box art
of the 1920s and 1930s.

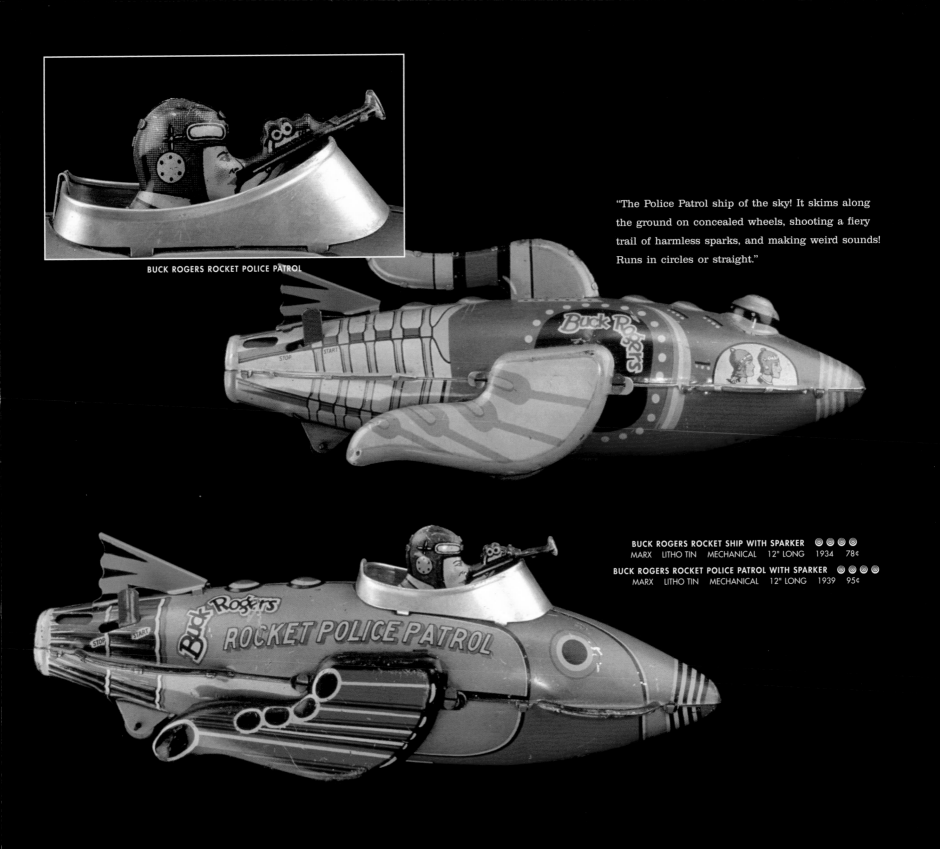

BUCK ROGERS ROCKET POLICE PATROL

"The Police Patrol ship of the sky! It skims along the ground on concealed wheels, shooting a fiery trail of harmless sparks, and making weird sounds! Runs in circles or straight."

**BUCK ROGERS ROCKET SHIP WITH SPARKER** ◎ ◎ ◎ ◎
MARX   LITHO TIN   MECHANICAL   12" LONG   1934   78¢

**BUCK ROGERS ROCKET POLICE PATROL WITH SPARKER** ◎ ◎ ◎ ◎
MARX   LITHO TIN   MECHANICAL   12" LONG   1939   95¢

When cocked and fired, the pistol makes a sort of "zap" sound and shows a reddish spark through the "electronic compression" view plate.

**BUCK ROGERS U-235 ATOMIC DISINTEGRATOR PISTOL**
DAISY    (COPPER COLOR FINISH, DUMMY COOLING FINS)    1934: 89¢    1935: 45¢

**BUCK ROGERS ROLLER SKATES**
CHICAGO ROLLER SKATE CO.    11" LONG    1930s

These heavy steel skates with their rocket shaped bow and red reflector stern rocketed many a lucky kid down 1930s city streets and sidewalks.

A handsome 25th century Buck Rogers outfit was available from Sackman Brothers. It consists of a suede-like helmet with isinglass goggles, the Atomic Pistol and holster, shirt, vest riveted with a leather Buck Rogers seal, and breeches and leather leggings. All for just $4.50.

"Buck Rogers fought the men from Mars in an outfit like this!"

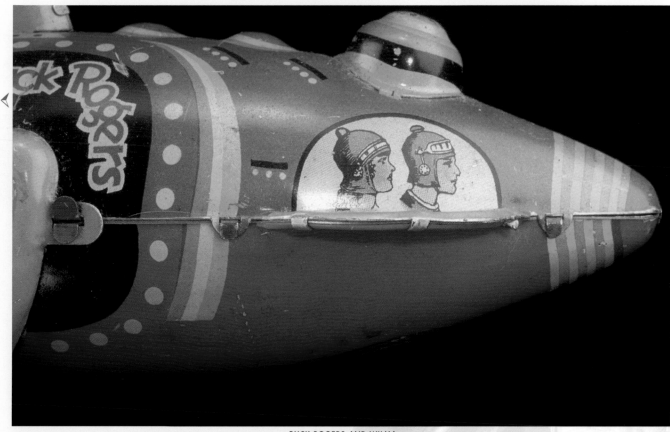

Buck Rogers represented the promise of the future in contrast to the reality of the era's Great Depression.

BUCK ROGERS AND WILMA

"To collect is to preserve things, valuable things, from neglect, from oblivion, or simply from the ignoble destiny

# cops and robbers

of being in someone else's collection rather than your own."

– SUSAN SONTAG

ON FEBRUARY 14, 1929, Chicago gangster
Al Capone ordered the execution of six
rivals in an event now known as the
St. Valentine's Day massacre.

"This American system of ours, call it
Americanism, call it Capitalism, call it
what you like, gives to each and every one
of us a great opportunity if we only seize it
with both hands and make the most of it."

— AL CAPONE

In 1934 bank robber "Pretty Boy Floyd"
was killed by the FBI, as were "Baby Face"
Nelson and John Dillinger.

Marx produced this sparks-shooting G-Man coupe in 1935. Exceptionally well made, it has a strong wind-up motor and is, to say the least — to child or nostalgic adult — colorful and vivid.

**G-MAN CAR**  MARX  PRESSED STEEL  MECHANICAL  1935  98¢
**DICK TRACY POP-UP BOOK**  BLUE RIBBON BOOKS  1935

"Join today's Public Heroes — the 'G' men who bravely enforce the law! Realistic 'Tommy' type machine gun. Wind the heavy clockwork spring motor...press the trigger and hear the rat-a-tat-tat machine gun noise. See the bright harmless sparks fly."

**TOMMY GUN NO.10**  HOGE  18" LONG  1937  98¢ (W/BATTERIES)
**G-MEN SECRET COMMUNICATIONS SET**  NEW YORK TOY & GAME CO.  1936
**G-MAN MACHINE GUN**  MARX  LITHO TIN  MECHANICAL  23" LONG  1935  94¢

DICK TRACY DETECTIVE SET    J. PRESSMAN & CO.    1944

Strong-jawed comic strip detective Dick Tracy was created by Chester Gould in 1931 to fight burgeoning organized crime in Depression-era America. As in real life, the bad guys — some of them not so bad — had colorful names — Flattop, Pruneface... B.O. Plenty...

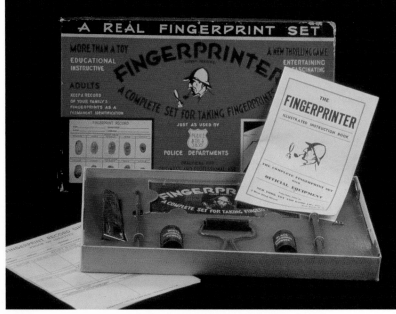

THE FINGERPRINTER    NEW YORK TOY AND GAME CO.    1930s

GANG BUSTERS GAME W/GATLING GUN    WHITMAN PUBLISHING CO.    1939

Aimed and cranked, this gatling-type gun shoots wood bullets at the bad guys.

1947: Marshall Plan proposed;
Dead Sea scrolls discovered

**DICK TRACY SIREN GUN** MARX PRESSED STEEL 8-1/2" LONG 1935 25¢
**DICK TRACY CANDY BAR WRAPPER**

▷ "A pull of the trigger and loud siren sound pierces the air!"

Crime-solving detectives, epitomized by the comic strip hero Dick Tracy, held special appeal during the age of gangsters, Prohibition, and the Depression.

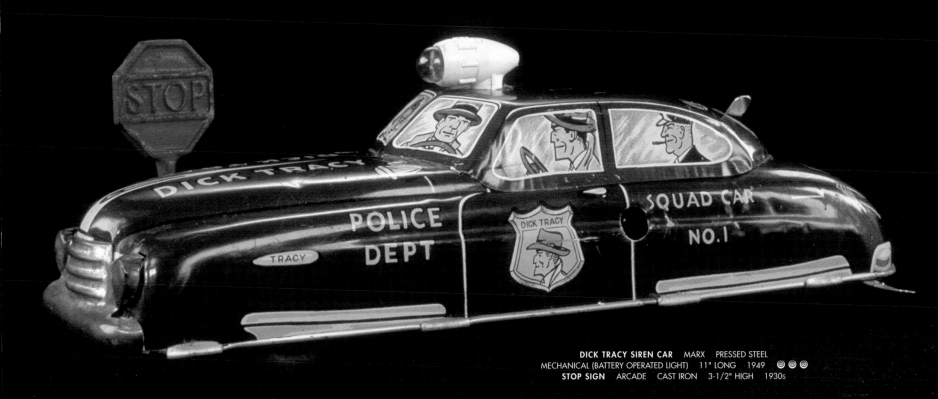

**DICK TRACY SIREN CAR** MARX PRESSED STEEL
MECHANICAL (BATTERY OPERATED LIGHT) 11" LONG 1949 ◎ ◎ ◎
**STOP SIGN** ARCADE CAST IRON 3-1/2" HIGH 1930s

**GANG BUSTERS TARGET**   BALDWIN MFG. CO.   LITHO TIN   1930s

**POLICE SET**   HALE HASS CORP.   1930s

**JOLLY ROBBERS SHOOTING GALLERY**   WILDER MANUFACTURING CO.   1929   $1

"Five bad looking robbers sitting on the fence in front of the tavern! Pop! One bites the dust. Bing! There goes another one; and if you are a real crack shot you'll get a perfect score with this dandy 17" break-action single barrel gun. Robbers are made of heavy cardboard and hinged to fence."

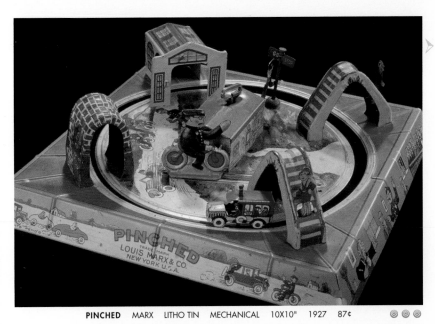

"Round the car goes, speeding ever faster.
Until stopped by the policeman!"

PINCHED   MARX   LITHO TIN   MECHANICAL   10X10"   1927   87¢   ◎ ◎ ◎

"An erratic-action traffic-police car that rears, turns in circles and
whose full-dress police officer, wholly confused by
everything that's going on, turns his head in circles too."

KOMICAL KOP   MARX   LITHO TIN   MECHANICAL   7-1/2" LONG   1930s   ◎ ◎ ◎

BLUTO CAR; POPEYE CAR   JAYMAR SPECIALTY CO.   LITHO PAPER ON WOOD PULL TOYS   1940s   ◎ ◎

These two cars are on an endless chase —
Does Popeye ever catch Bluto? And then what happens?!

**RADIO POLICE GAME** WHITMAN PUBLISHING CO. 1930s 19¢ ◎ ◎ ◎

**INDIAN 4-CYLINDER MOTORCYCLE WITH REMOVABLE POLICEMAN** ◎ ◎ ◎ ◎ ◎
HUBLEY CAST IRON 9" LONG 1930s DUDLEY MADDOX COLLECTION

**INDIAN 2-CYLINDER MOTORCYCLE W/SIDECAR AND REMOVABLE POLICEMAN** ◎ ◎ ◎ ◎
HUBLEY CAST IRON 9" LONG 1930s PAUL AND KATIE HEDBURN COLLECTION

➤A prized toy in its day,
rare and valuable today.

"The funniest policeman you ever saw. He changes the expression of his face from a happy smile to a frown, then cheers up again as he shuffles along with his arms swinging and his body swaying."

MOTORCYCLES   MARX   LITHO TIN   MECHANICAL   8" LONG   1930s   ◎ ◎ ◎

"He's just learning and takes lots of spills...but gets right up without help! Rides along nicely awhile...then falls again!"

MOTORCYCLE W/SIDE CAR   MARX   LITHO TIN   8-1/2" LONG   1949   EACH: ◎ ◎ ◎
POLICE TIPOVER MOTORCYCLE   MARX   LITHO TIN   8" LONG   1933   34¢
ROOKIE MOTORCYCLE COP   MARX   LITHO TIN   8" LONG   49¢   1935
MOTORCYCLE COP   UNIQUE ART   LITHO TIN   8" LONG   1930s

OFFICER 666   MARX   LITHO TIN   MECHANICAL   11" HIGH   1931   48¢   ◎ ◎ ◎ ◎

"Inside each of us is
a spiritual vacuum
and it's the task of our
lifetime to fill it.

# cowboys and indians

The creation and the
collecting of art is a
necessity, not a luxury
and without art the
soul withers and
the civilization dies."

— ROBERT LESSER

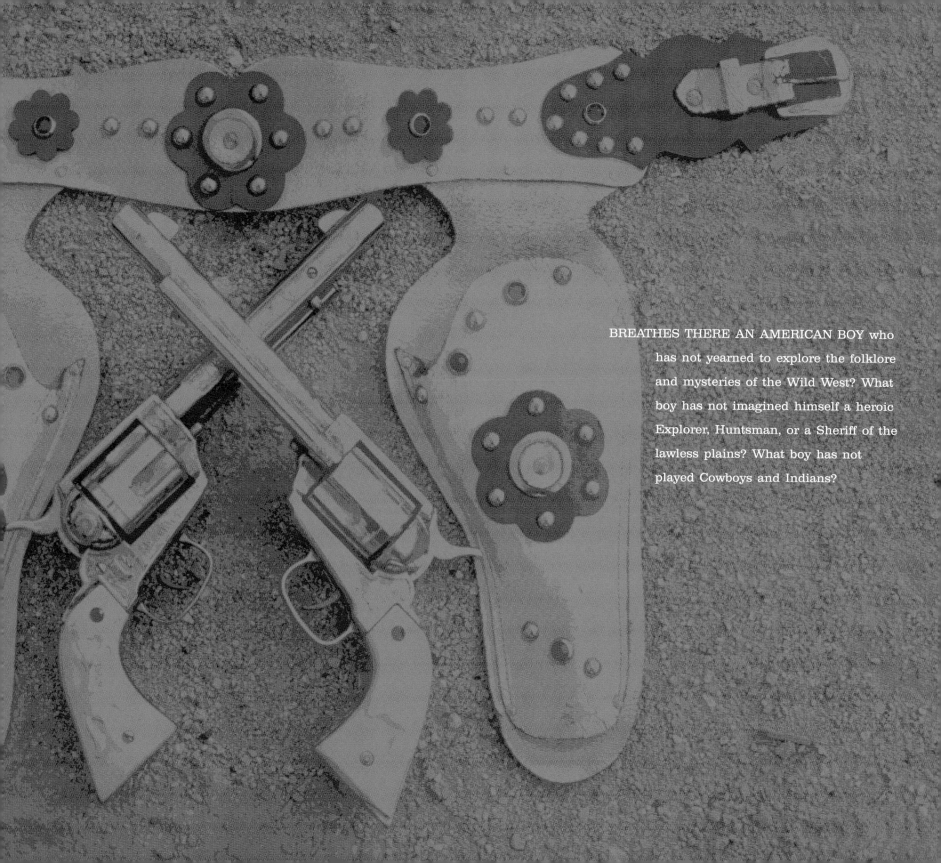

BREATHES THERE AN AMERICAN BOY who has not yearned to explore the folklore and mysteries of the Wild West? What boy has not imagined himself a heroic Explorer, Huntsman, or a Sheriff of the lawless plains? What boy has not played Cowboys and Indians?

**FRONTIER SET**  KEYSTONE  59 PIECES  1934  $1

**WESTERN FRONTIER SETS**  MARX  LITHO TIN  EARLY 1950s
**ST. PAUL AND PACIFIC RR PASSENGER CARS**  MARX  EARLY 1950s

The spectacular "Wild West Show" of "Buffalo Bill"
Cody, featuring sharp-shooting Annie Oakley and,
for a time, Indian Chief Sitting Bull, thrilled audiences
across America and Europe.

**BUFFALO BILL COWBOY**
MARX    LITHO TIN    MECHANICAL    c1928

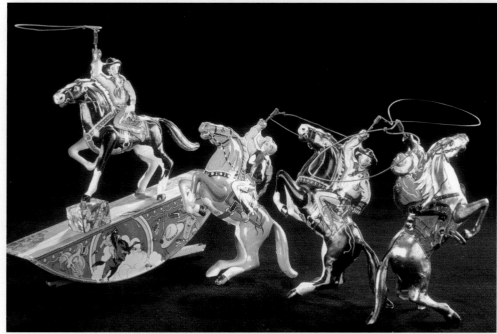

"A fiery horse with the speed of light, a cloud of dust, and a hearty 'Hi-ho Silver!', 'the Lone Ranger rides again!" With "The William Tell Overture" playing in the background, the "Lone Ranger" debuted on the radio in 1933.

When wound, these horses prance (the Range Rider rocks) and the cowboys, riding the Western plains bringing law and order to an untamed frontier (or possibly a cattle stampede), spin their lariats.

| **RANGE RIDER** | MARX | LITHO TIN | MECHANICAL | 11" LONG | 1941 | | EACH: ◉ ◉ ◉ |
| **COWBOY** | MARX | LITHO TIN | MECHANICAL | 7-1/2" HIGH | 1941 | 29¢ |
| **COWBOY** | MARX | LITHO TIN | MECHANICAL | 7-1/2" HIGH | 1941 | 29¢ |
| **LONE RANGER** | MARX | LITHO TIN | MECHANICAL | | 1938 | 25¢ |

"Instead of a bucking bull, a bucking cowboy!"

1948: Ghandi assassinated.

**WHOOPEE COWBOY**  MARX   LITHO TIN   MECHANICAL   8" LONG   1932   59¢   ◉ ◉ ◉

Comic strip hero Red Ryder was the lanky good-natured ◁
cowboy who appeared in hundreds of newspapers in the
1930s. He also had a short-lived radio program.

RED RYDER GAME    WHITMAN PUBLISHING CO.    1939    25¢    ◎ ◎ ◎

LINDSTROM'S INDIAN CHIEF BAGATELLE
LINDSTROM    LITHO TIN    1930s    ◎ ◎ ◎

▷ Beautiful (and rare), this bagatelle game
can almost be considered educational.

◢ Singing cowboy Roy Rogers, with his wife Dale Evans and horse Trigger, were perennial stars of stage and screen.

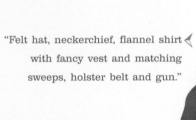

**ROY ROGERS GUN AND HOLSTER** ◉ ◉ ◉
CLASSY PRODUCTS CORP.   1957   $4.95

**RED RYDER BAGATELLE**   GOTHAM   1950   ◉ ◉ ◉

"Felt hat, neckerchief, flannel shirt ◁
with fancy vest and matching
sweeps, holster belt and gun."

**COWBOY SUIT AND MANNEQUIN**
SACKMAN BROTHERS   1930s – 1940s
◉ ◉ ◉

**STALLION .45 GUNS**  HUBLEY  1951  ERNEST MILES COLLECTION
**HOLSTERS**  ESQUIRE CO.

1948: Soviet forces blockade West Berlin.

**GUN**  HUBLEY  CAST IRON  1954          EACH: ◎ ◎
**GUN**  KENTON  CAST IRON  1951
**GUN**  HUBLEY  CAST IRON  1958

"'Tony' is an exact miniature of Tom Mix's famous movie horse.
A long sweeping rocker prevents tipping from backward or forward motion.
Equipped with strong bridle rein and Tom Mix lariat."

TOM MIX ROCKING HORSE  MENGEL CO.   40" HIGH   1939   $5.25  ◎ ◎ ◎ ◎

Both the head and arms of this Mickey are articulated — podner!

A Ralston cereal premium (a box top and a dime), this Tom Mix wood gun has a revolving cylinder.

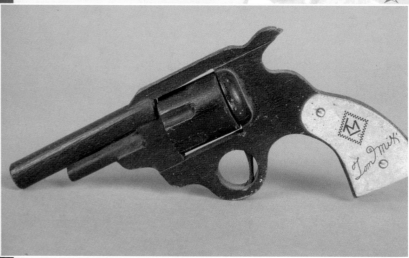

**TOM MIX PISTOL** (RADIO PREMIUM)    WOOD (REVOLVING CYLINDER)    PAPER HANDLE

**MICKEY MOUSE COWBOY**    KNICKERBOCKER DOLL CO.    COMPOSITION
ARTICULATED HEAD AND ARMS    9-1/2" HIGH    1936    PAUL AND KATIE HEDBURN COLLECTION

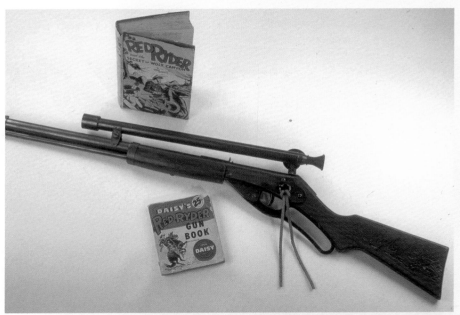

**RED RYDER NO.111 B-B GUN WITH IRON COCKING LEVER AND ATTACHABLE SCOPE**
DAISY MANUFACTURING CO.   1940
**DAISY'S RED RYDER GUN BOOK**
**RED RYDER SECRETS OF WOLF CANYON**   BIG LITTLE BOOK   WHITMAN   1930s   10¢

"Here's Buck Jones' own air rifle — built by
Daisy to the famous Cowboy Movie Star's own
specifications. Barrel and sights tested for
accurate shooting at the factory. Slide action
with polished natural finish pistol grip stock.
Burned in sundial, set-in floating compass.
Gun blue finish barrel, engraved receiver."

**BUCK JONES AIR RIFLE**
60-SHOT REPEATER   DAISY MANUFACTURING CO.   1934   $2.74
**BUCK JONES THE FIGHTING RANGERS**
BIG LITTLE BOOK WHITMAN   1930s   10¢

"A collector draws objects out of the forgotten past or scattered present... Order is created out of chaos, history is remade; fate is reshaped.

# prejudice and racism

Within a treasured collection, objects are redeemed; they are granted freedom from the mundane."

– WALTER BENJAMIN

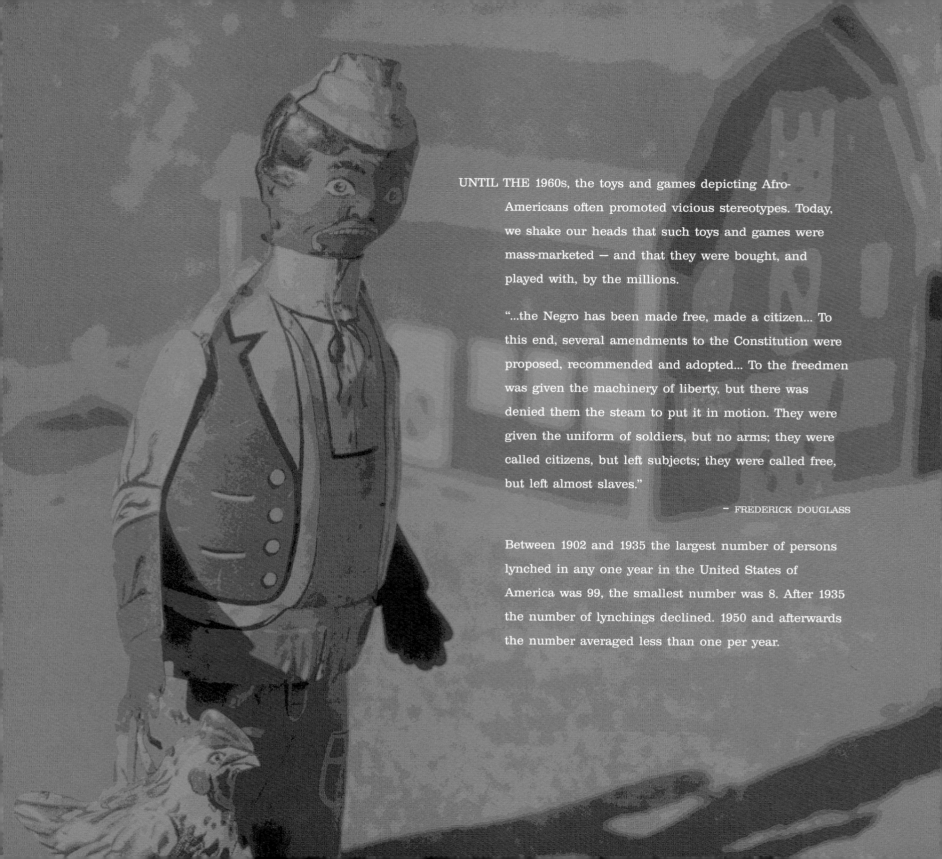

UNTIL THE 1960s, the toys and games depicting Afro-Americans often promoted vicious stereotypes. Today, we shake our heads that such toys and games were mass-marketed — and that they were bought, and played with, by the millions.

"...the Negro has been made free, made a citizen... To this end, several amendments to the Constitution were proposed, recommended and adopted... To the freedmen was given the machinery of liberty, but there was denied them the steam to put it in motion. They were given the uniform of soldiers, but no arms; they were called citizens, but left subjects; they were called free, but left almost slaves."

— FREDERICK DOUGLASS

Between 1902 and 1935 the largest number of persons lynched in any one year in the United States of America was 99, the smallest number was 8. After 1935 the number of lynchings declined. 1950 and afterwards the number averaged less than one per year.

**MAUDE AND SAM**   ALL-FAIR   LITHO LAMINATED CARDBOARD   19" LONG   1928   95¢   ◎ ◎ ◎

"Maude has a kick she learned before the war and any youngster will give an involuntary grunt when 'Sammy' comes down with a thud on balky Maude's back."

**SAMBO TARGET**   WYANDOTTE   LITHO TIN   1930s   ◎ ◎ ◎

"Object of game: To toss Bean bags thru the holes (Mose, Sambo, Rastus) in target."

"Rules: Stand six to twelve feet from target. Each player throws the three bean bags in turn and keeps score. Bean bag must go thru hole to score. Bag hanging in hole does not score."

1949: Television takes hold.

BEAN-EM   ALL-FAIR   1931   95¢   ◎ ◎ ◎ ◎

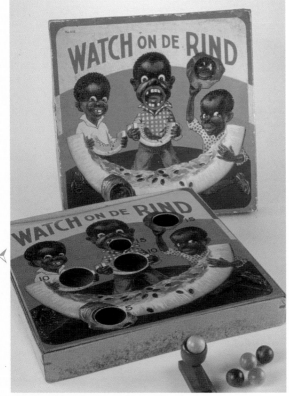

The graphics and the jeering title of this game speak volumes about the status of Afro-Americans in America. The game appeared during the Depression in 1931 and was sold in the dime stores for 25¢.

WATCH ON DE RIND GAME   ALL-FAIR   1931   25¢   ◎ ◎ ◎ ◎

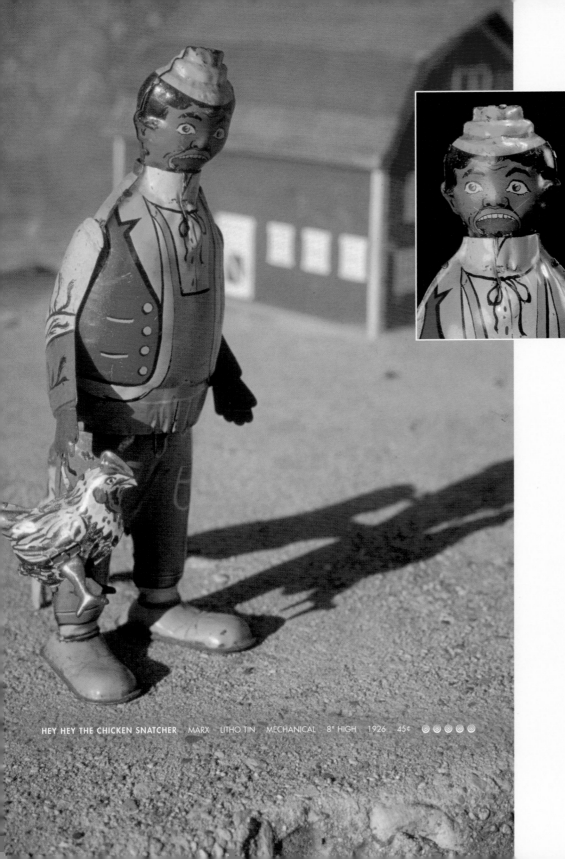

HEY HEY THE CHICKEN SNATCHER   MARX   LITHO TIN   MECHANICAL   8" HIGH   1926   45¢   ◎ ◎ ◎ ◎ ◎

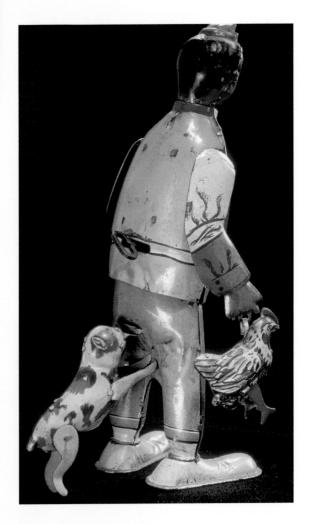

"When 'Shep' and Sambo both want
the chicken you're sure there's going
to be lots of excitement and fun."

**MAMMY**   LINDSTROM   LITHO TIN   MECHANICAL   1930s

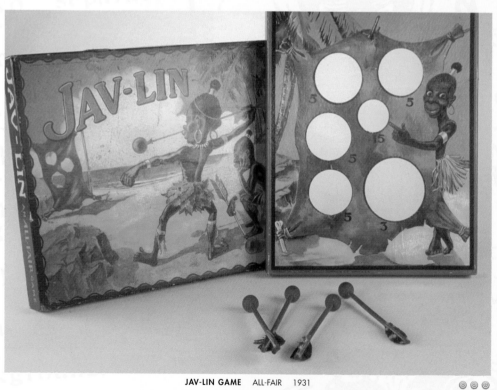

**JAV-LIN GAME**   ALL-FAIR   1931

Whether one considers this a racist toy or not, this is one of the all-time great toys. Its innumerable parts come together to create both comedy and spirit as the wind-up car moves along, stalls, shakes, jiggling Amos, the Open Air Taxi Company's driver, and cigar-smoking back-seat driver President Andrew Brown, then moves jerkily on. A fabulous, fabulous toy. When it came on the market in 1930 it sold for 95¢ (it was not a good seller). A year later, the depressed economy growing ever worse, Marx lowered the retail price to 48¢.

**AMOS 'N' ANDY OPEN-AIR TAXI**   MARX   LITHO TIN   7-3/4" LONG   1930   95¢ (1931-1932, 48¢)

**CHARLESTON TRIO**   MARX   LITHO TIN   MECHANICAL   10" HIGH   1926   47¢
**ALABAMA COON JIGGER**   STRAUSS   LITHO TIN   MECHANICAL   10" HIGH   1921   59¢
**SPIC AND SPAN "THE HAM'S WHAT AM"**   MARX   LITHO TIN   MECHANICAL   10" HIGH   1924   69¢
**DAPPER DAN COON JIGGER**   MARX   LITHO TIN   MECHANICAL   9-1/2" HIGH   1924   49¢
**JAZZBO JIM**   UNIQUE ART   LITHO TIN   MECHANICAL   9" HIGH   1925   45¢

1949: Rodgers' and Hammerstein's *South Pacific*
premiers on Broadway.

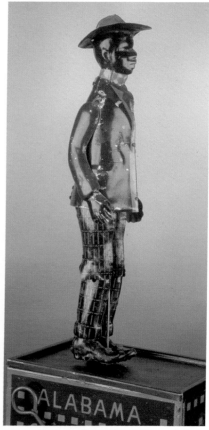

**ALABAMA COON JIGGER**

CHARLESTON TRIO

"Wind the strong spring and the Charleston trio start their snappy performance. How that big fellow can dance! Watch the little man fiddle away while the dog rises up on his hind legs keeping time."

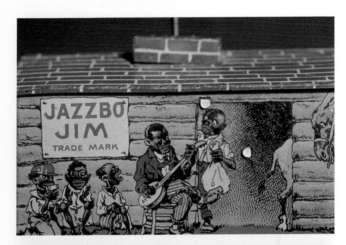

JAZZBO JIM HOUSING

SPIC AND SPAN

"Spic makes the music; Span amuses the audience."

"Beauty makes it
seem as if the object
we are gazing at were
perfectly adapted to
our understanding,

# carnival! the circus comes to town!

as if there were some
unexpected harmony
between the mind of the
observer and the object
being observed."

– EDWARD ROTHSTEIN

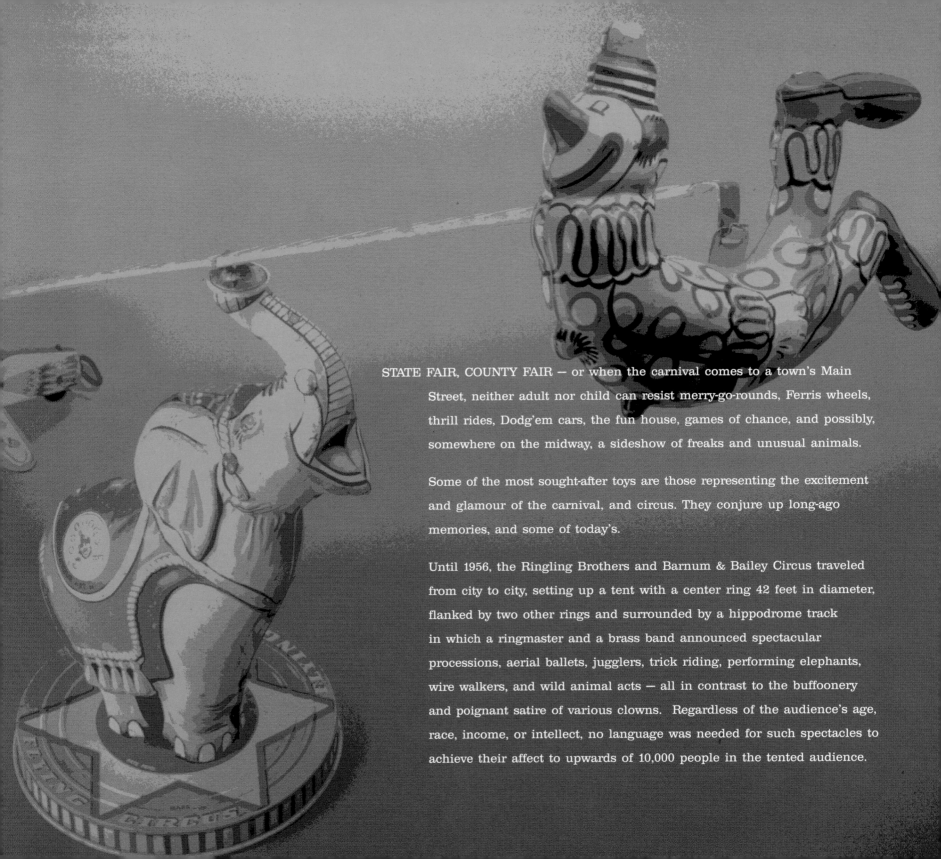

STATE FAIR, COUNTY FAIR — or when the carnival comes to a town's Main Street, neither adult nor child can resist merry-go-rounds, Ferris wheels, thrill rides, Dodg'em cars, the fun house, games of chance, and possibly, somewhere on the midway, a sideshow of freaks and unusual animals.

Some of the most sought-after toys are those representing the excitement and glamour of the carnival, and circus. They conjure up long-ago memories, and some of today's.

Until 1956, the Ringling Brothers and Barnum & Bailey Circus traveled from city to city, setting up a tent with a center ring 42 feet in diameter, flanked by two other rings and surrounded by a hippodrome track in which a ringmaster and a brass band announced spectacular processions, aerial ballets, jugglers, trick riding, performing elephants, wire walkers, and wild animal acts — all in contrast to the buffoonery and poignant satire of various clowns. Regardless of the audience's age, race, income, or intellect, no language was needed for such spectacles to achieve their affect to upwards of 10,000 people in the tented audience.

**ROLLER COASTER WITH TWO CARS**   CHEIN   LITHO TIN   MECHANICAL   20" LONG   1949   $2.98
**GIANT ROLLER COASTER**   REEVES   LITHO TIN   MECHANICAL   1927   $5
**SKEETER BUG**   BUFFALO TOYS   PRESSED STEEL   MECHANICAL   9-1/4" LONG   1948

**HERCULES FERRIS WHEEL**   CHEIN   LITHO TIN   MECHANICAL   16-1/2" HIGH   1930s
**CONEY ISLAND THE GIANT DIP**   MANUFACTURER UNKNOWN
18" X 6" OVERALL   13" TOWER WITH 4 PLANES   1929

1949: The Communist
　　　　People's Republic is
proclaimed in China.

This unusual action toy is an outstanding one. It operates without winding. One pull of lever in its base sends it whirling steadily around, while the music tinkles merrily, horses trot, and planes fly.

**MERRY-GO-ROUNDS**  WOLVERINE   LITHO TIN   11" DIAMETER   1928   98¢
(MERRY-GO-ROUND IN BACKGROUND MADE IN 1936)

These plaster of Paris (chalkware) statuettes, produced in the hundreds of thousands, were awarded as prizes at carnival and amusement park games of chance or skill from the 1930s to the1950s. Today, however, they are becoming harder and harder to find — especially in unbroken, unchipped condition.

**CARNIVAL CHALKWARE:** SUPERMAN,  PINOCCHIO, POPEYE,   EACH: ◎ ◎
LONE RANGER, WIMPY, SNOW WHITE, DONALD DUCK, CHARLIE MCCARTHY, DOPEY,
FELIX, FERDINAND THE BULL, JIGGS AND MAGGIE, BONGO

A wonderfully elaborate, fully operating toy incorporating many of the rides available at carnivals.

**WYANDOTTE CARNIVAL**
WYANDOTTE   LITHO TIN   MECHANICAL   1940   $2.50   ROBERT MANELLO COLLECTION

Of all American toy companies, Chein produced unusually large and lustrous carnival-ride toys.

**RIDE A ROCKET**
CHEIN   LITHO TIN   MECHANICAL   18-1/2" LONG   1952

This toy replicates the "whip" of certain real-life carnival rides.

**PLAYLAND WHIP**   CHEIN   LITHO TIN   MECHANICAL   1950s

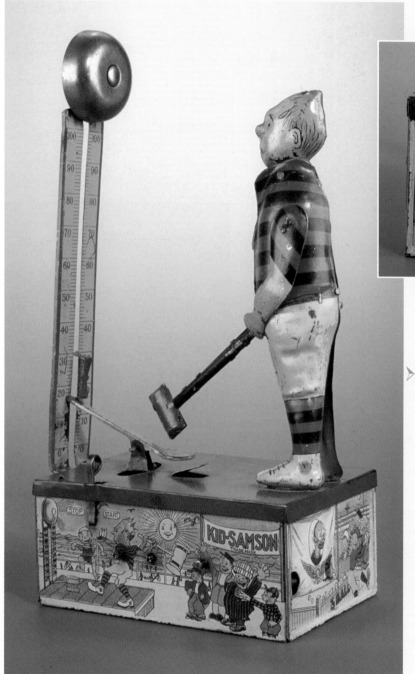

**KID SAMSON**   SELRITE   LITHO TIN   MECHANICAL   7-1/2" HIGH   1927

**DETAIL** OF THE KID SAMSON TOY PORTRAYING IN CARTOON FORM A REAL-LIFE SCENE.

› Step right up young man!
Show the lady how strong you are!

1950: North Korea invades South Korea.

If the dare-devil at the top of the ramp steers his car properly, he will race down the ramp, fly off, hook himself on the raised bar, and spin to a stop.

**JUMPIN' JITNEY**   WOLVERINE   PRESSED STEEL AND TIN   1929

"Even Dad will want to play! There's a stationary 12-inch metal upper target and a 7-inch swinging target below, run on a clock-spring motor. A steel target pistol with six rubber suction darts is included."

**SWINGING TARGET**
MARX   LITHO TIN   MECHANICAL   1949   $1.39

"Look! Here he comes, racing down the ramp in his metal racecar! Then, zoom, he loops the loop and dashes madly across the floor."

**DARE DEVIL DICK**   NOVEL PRODUCTS CO.   PRESSED STEEL   16" HIGH   1947   89¢

Ducks move across
the line of fire.

**SHOOTING ARCADE TARGET** KNICKERBOCKER CO. BATTERY-OPERATED 1947 89¢ ◎

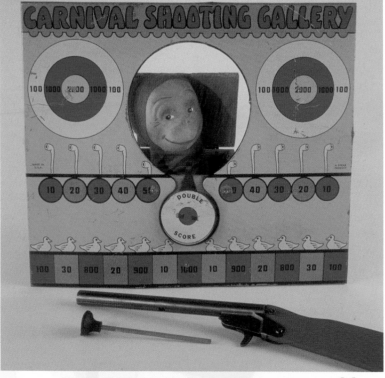

Monkey disappears when
hit by rubber suction-cup
shooting pistol.

**CARNIVAL SHOOTING GALLERY TARGET** SPEAR CO. 1930s ◎ ◎

CARNIVAL TARGET   UNIQUE ART   MECHANICAL   14" LONG   1930s   $1.98

"This all-metal, highly lithographed miniature shooting gallery has, besides many numbered stationary targets, two moving targets driven by a key-wound spring motor. One of these is a revolving disc in the back, the other a line of small ducks that move across the line of fire in single file."

White-hatted Tom Mix, a radio and movie star — "The World's Champion Cowboy" — formed his own circus and played command performances before the crown heads of Europe.

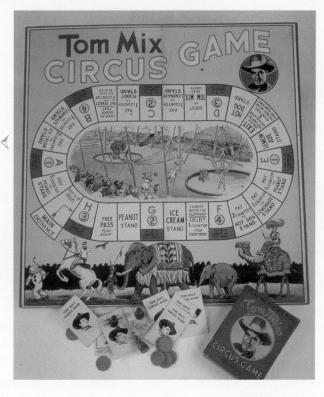

TOM MIX CIRCUS GAME   PARKER BROS.

The Hubley bandwagon, 30-inches long,
with four horses, a driver, and
eight musicians, is extremely rare.

**ROYAL CIRCUS BANDWAGON**   HUBLEY   CAST IRON   1919-1926   PAUL AND KATIE HEDBURN COLLECTION

"Collapsible tent decorated with flags of all nations and equipped with wire trapeze and ring. Also a pretty red divided curtain in back on gilt pole and trimmed with gold fiber fringe. Wood base with sawdust glued to it with red wood ring in center."

**HUMPTY-DUMPY CIRCUS**  SCHOENHUT   WOOD, PRINTED CLOTH
FULL-SIZE ANIMALS 8" TO 9" LONG; FIGURES, 8" HIGH   1903 TO 1935

Collectors vie for Schoenhut circus performers, animals, and accessories. They transcend "toys." They belong in the category of folk art. They are timeless, American originals.

**LION**   SCHOENHUT   WOOD WITH GLASS EYES
8" LONG   c1906   PAUL AND KATIE HEDBURN COLLECTION

**TIGER**   SCHOENHUT   WOOD WITH GLASS EYES
8" LONG   c1906   PAUL AND KATIE HEDBURN COLLECTION

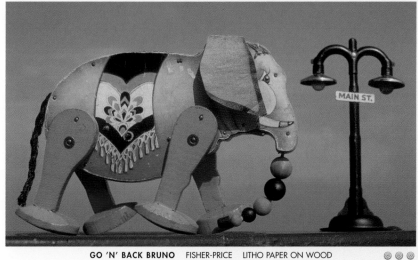

GO 'N' BACK BRUNO   FISHER-PRICE   LITHO PAPER ON WOOD
MECHANICAL   8-3/4" LONG   1931   $1.50

Jumbo plods along at a determined gait, body swaying from side to side and trunk swinging back and forth. Motor-driven mechanical wood toy that walks forward and backwards like a live, conscious animal.

CIRCUS CAGE   SCHOENHUT   WOOD   9" LONG

GREATEST SHOW ON EARTH   LINDSTROM   LITHO TIN   MECHANICAL
29" LONG   1931   $1.48   DAVID E. STOERMER COLLECTION

"Mechanical Barnum & Bailey Circus wagon, which when wound up will go 25 feet on one winding. It is equipped with a cage of animals that can be taken off the chassis and opened. When walking, the elephant's legs move, as if the pulling power was in the elephant."

LION CAGE TRUCK   STRAUSS   LITHO TIN   MECHANICAL   10-1/2" LONG   1926   89¢   ◎ ◎ ◎ ◎

1951: The U. S. begins
nuclear testing in Nevada.

With its aerodynamic
cab design, embossed
wooden wheels, and
removable rear door
panels on the cages, this
is a spectacular circus
toy, one of the best
Wyandotte produced.

CIRCUS TRUCK AND TRAILER   WYANDOTTE   LITHO TIN AND PRESSED STEEL   19" LONG   1936   50¢   ◎ ◎ ◎ ◎

An elegant circus pull toy: the seal
balances a revolving ball on his nose
as the polar bear strikes the bell.

BEAR AND SEAL BELL PULL TOY   WOLVERINE   LITHO TIN   1926   ◎ ◎ ◎

This clown's car is,
without doubt, a crazy car.

**WHAT'S IT?**
STRAUSS   LITHO TIN   MECHANICAL   1927   SAM JOHNSON COLLECTION

Both plane and clown —
they're airborne!

**FLYING CIRCUS**   UNIQUE ART   LITHO TIN   MECHANICAL   1947

"They'll float through the air with the greatest of ease — and do a world of tricks! Grand circus set including metal bars and poles, trapezes and 7 cast iron clowns you can make perform as you wish! There's a net to catch the clowns when they fall."

**CLEVER CLOWNS**   GREY IRON   18" HIGH   1936   $1.50   ◎ ◎ ◎

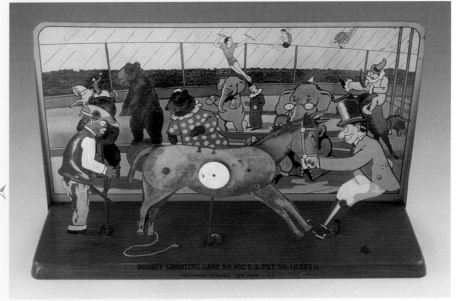

Cock the donkey's leg. When the donkey is struck with a pistol's rubber suction-cup missive, the donkey kicks the poor groom. As though it's the groom's fault!

**DONKEY SHOOTING GAME**   STRAUSS   PRESSED STEEL   1926   ◎ ◎ ◎ ◎

"The monkey climbs the ◁ wire! The ringmaster snaps his whip! The clown turns a somersault! The lion and the elephant perform! And all at the same time!"

**RING-A-LING CIRCUS** MARX ◎ ◎ ◎ ◎
LITHO TIN MECHANICAL 7-1/2" DIAMETER 1925 89¢

The wind-up clown ◁ demonstrates his remarkable prowess with the celluloid punching bag.

**CLOWN PUNCHER** CHEIN ◎ ◎ ◎ ◎
LITHO TIN MECHANICAL 7-1/2" HIGH 1937

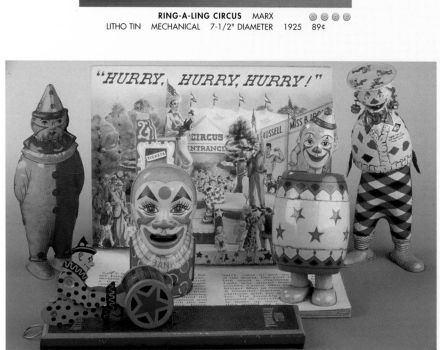

**JOLLY JUMPUP CIRCUS BOOK** McLAUGHLIN BROS. ◎
**LINDSTROM "JOHNNY" CLOWN** ◎
**CLOWN BANK** CHEIN 1937 10¢ ◎
**CLOWN IN A BARREL** CHEIN 1937 ◎ ◎
**TOM TWIST THE FUNNY CLOWN** STRAUSS LITHO TIN MECHANICAL 1932 ◎ ◎
**TUMBLIN' TOM** MANUFACTURER UNKNOWN ◎ ◎

▷ Pull the string and Tom turns head over heels. Or heels over head.

**"JOHNNY" CLOWN** EACH: ◎ ◎
LINDSTROM LITHO TIN MECHANICAL 6" HIGH 1930s
**TUMBLIN' TOM** (STRING PULL ACTION) MANUFACTURER UNKNOWN
LITHO TIN 8-1/2" LONG 1930s

**TOM TWIST THE FUNNY CLOWN** EACH: ◎ ◎ ◎
STRAUSS LITHO TIN MECHANICAL 1932
**CLOWN IN BARREL** CHEIN LITHO TIN MECHANICAL 1930s

**CLOWN BANK** CHEIN LITHO TIN 1937 10¢ ◎ ◎

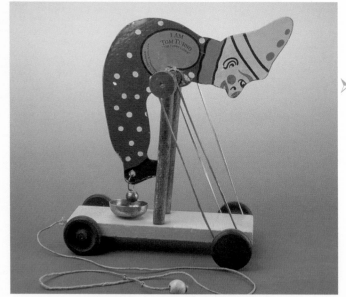

"Tom Turno — snappy cardboard clown tumbles over his bar and hits the bell on the platform as he is pulled along."

**TOM TURNO**   NEWTON & THOMAS MFG. CO.
LITHO CARDBOARD AND WOOD   1926   25¢

"A fascinating action occurs when the string is pulled. The monkey climbs up the string with the aid of his hands and feet. When the tension is released, he performs the same action downward."

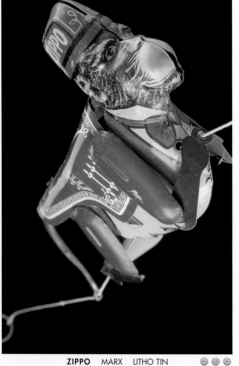

This performer not only does handstands and loops, he does them backwards.

**ZIPPO**   MARX   LITHO TIN
9" LONG   1930   25¢

EZE ARTIST   WYANDOTTE   LITHO TIN   MECHANICAL   1930s

**CIRCUS PLAY SET** (FIGURES SHOWN NOT INCLUDED)   MARX   LITHO TIN   1953

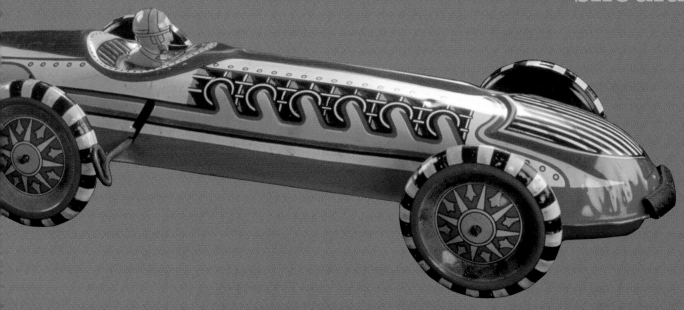

"Toys are important in helping to form character, but I am not much for educational toys.

# the sporting scene

First and foremost, toys should be fun."

— LOUIS MARX

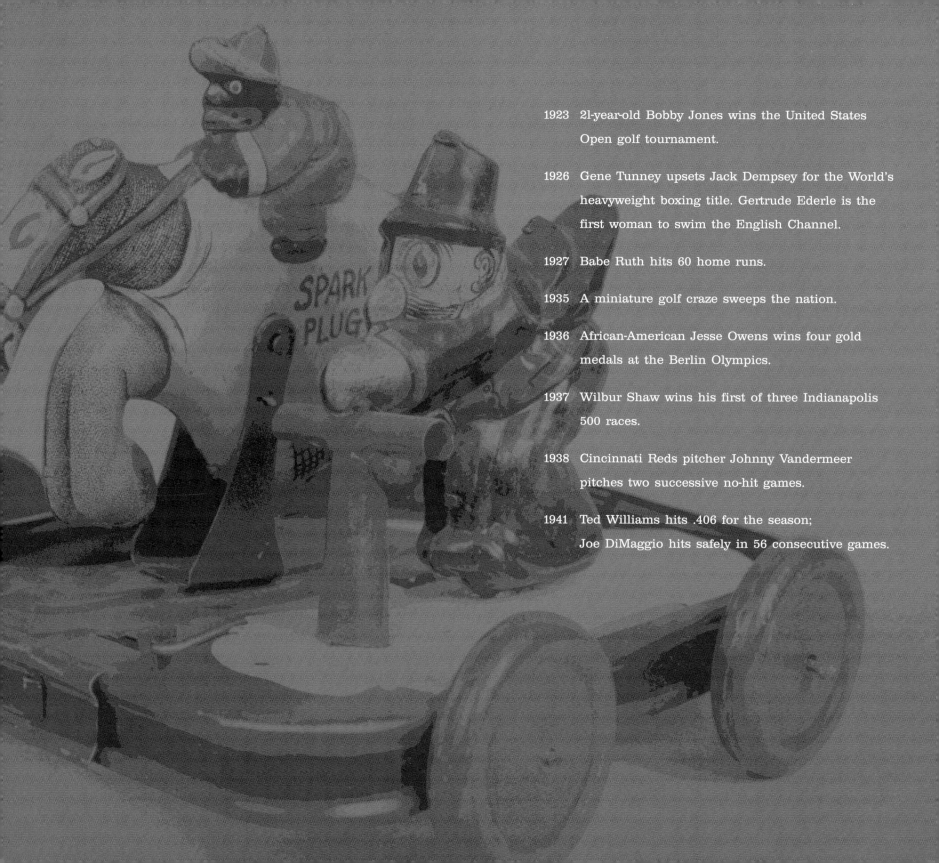

1923 21-year-old Bobby Jones wins the United States Open golf tournament.

1926 Gene Tunney upsets Jack Dempsey for the World's heavyweight boxing title. Gertrude Ederle is the first woman to swim the English Channel.

1927 Babe Ruth hits 60 home runs.

1935 A miniature golf craze sweeps the nation.

1936 African-American Jesse Owens wins four gold medals at the Berlin Olympics.

1937 Wilbur Shaw wins his first of three Indianapolis 500 races.

1938 Cincinnati Reds pitcher Johnny Vandermeer pitches two successive no-hit games.

1941 Ted Williams hits .406 for the season; Joe DiMaggio hits safely in 56 consecutive games.

It's really a roller-coaster, of course, but dressed up in winter garb, why not call it a Ski Ride?

**SKI RIDE ROLLER COASTER**   CHEIN   LITHO TIN   MECHANICAL   20" LONG   1952 ◎◎◎

"Keep in trim with indoor Horse Shoes. Pony size, 4 soft rubber shoes will not scratch or mar your floors. Get the whole family into a tournament or have a horseshoe pitching contest at your next party. Use this set indoor or outdoors."

**PITCH 'EM HORSE SHOES**   WOLVERINE   ◎
1920   87¢

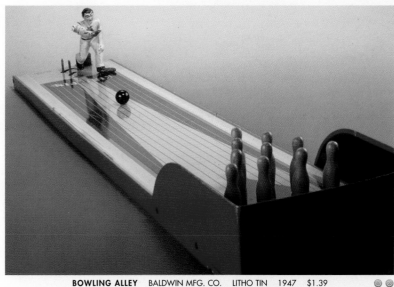

The bowler's arm is cocked and, when released, sends his ball toward the pins in hopes of a strike, not a gutter ball!

Before World War II, bowling alleys were for the most part unglamorous, downscale venues with grubby pin-boys and a tavern next door. But with postwar prosperity, raffish bowling alleys — as well as pool halls — where workingmen formerly gathered to drink and relax were now swept up into the respectable, family-oriented world of Mr. Clean.

**BOWLING ALLEY**   BALDWIN MFG. CO.   LITHO TIN   1947   $1.39 ◎◎

These two too-cool guys are actually pretty good.

Only now and then do they "scratch" the ball.

**POOL PLAYERS**   RANGER STEEL PRODUCTS   LITHO TIN   MECHANICAL   1945

**LITTLE CHAMPION POOL TABLE** AMERICANA GAME & TOY CORP. 16-1/2" LONG 1926 $1.29 ◎ ◎

➤ "Made of heavy gauge metal, lithographed beautiful mahogany color. Covered with real green billiard cloth. Consists of 16 marbles, 2 spring cues and one metal triangle."

**STRONG MAN** SCHOENHUT WOOD ◎ ◎ ◎
8" HIGH PAUL AND KATIE HEDBURN COLLECTION

STANDARD MODEL
No. 41
Patented

Length, 29
Minimum S
Carton, 1
Weight, 10

A SPLENDID sporting model, preferred by adults. Grained in mahogany-finish wood—with partitions between discs to match. Horses and jockeys are well moulded in 6 different colors. Discs and flags correspond in color with the horses. Base bright green. Appearance of latest models is enhanced by metal corners. The entire effect is strikingly attractive. Works on the same principle as Model No. 40. Operates to satisfaction always. **{ 285 }** THE SPORTING SCENE

Popeye trains ferociously,
if not stiffly, with a
celluloid punching bag.

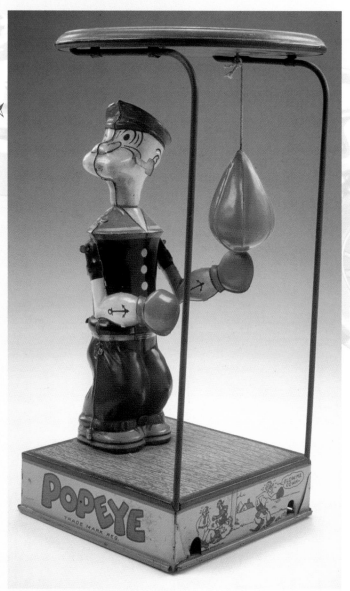

**POPEYE BAG PUNCHER**   CHEIN   LITHO TIN   ◎ ◎ ◎ ◎ ◎
MECHANICAL   9-1/2" HIGH   1932   50¢

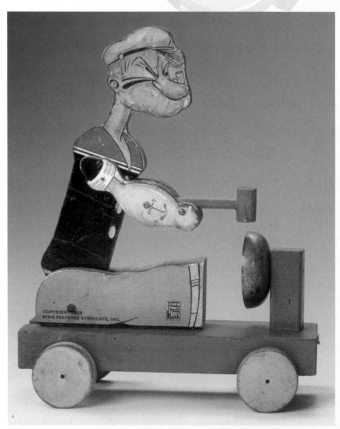

**POP-EYE**   FISHER-PRICE   LITHO PAPER ON WOOD; BELL   1935   ◎ ◎ ◎ ◎

Furious action! Round after round Popeye and Bluto fight, and when the bell rings which one will be knocked down no one can know.

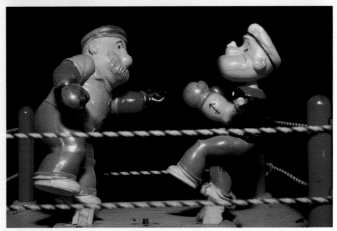

**POPEYE THE CHAMP**  MARX  LITHO TIN (CELLULOID FIGURES)
MECHANICAL  7" SQUARE  1935  98¢

BIRD'S EYE BAGATELLE   DURABLE TOY AND NOVELTY CO.   c1938   ◎ ◎

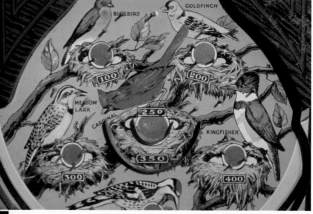

1952: Jonas Salk
discovers vaccine for polio.

When any one of these ducks are hit, ◁
they fall away revealing the score.

DUCK HUNTING TARGET   WYANDOTTE TOYS   LITHO TIN   1930s   ◎ ◎

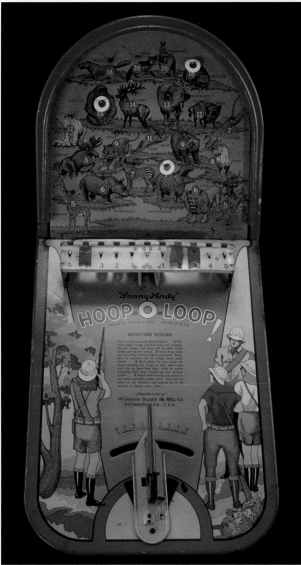

Animals are printed in colors on the raised section. There is a hook for each animal. The gun mounted at the front hurls rings over hooks. Each has a different score.

**HOOP-O-LOOP**  WOLVERINE  LITHO TIN
18" LONG  1935  45¢

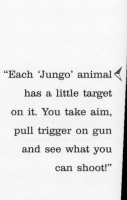

"Each 'Jungo' animal has a little target on it. You take aim, pull trigger on gun and see what you can shoot!"

**JUNGO**  LITHO TIN  1933  $1

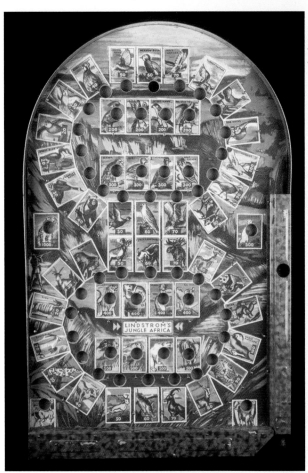

**LINDSTROM'S JUNGLE AFRICA BAGATELLE**
LINDSTROM   LITHO TIN   1930s

Another unusually detailed lithographed bagatelle from Lindstrom.

"The sport of kings! Six horses race up the track with every one of them having an equal chance to win. The flag goes up as each horse reaches the finish line. No two races finish alike. Just spin fly-wheel with heavy cord, shaft drives steel balls against horses, advancing them along tracks. Great party game. Any number can play. Handsome mahogany wood finish frame."

**GEE-WIZ**   WOLVERINE   METAL, WOOD   29" LONG   1927   $13

Who would have thought
that Popeye, a sailor,
could ride a horse?

**POPEYE COWBOY**   FISHER-PRICE   LITHO PAPER ON WOOD   1937

**BARNEY GOOGLE RACING TOY**   NIFTY   LITHO TIN   8" LONG   1924

"Barney, on a scooter,
endlessly races Sunshine
and Sparkplug."

The annual all-American Soap Box Derby — "Boydom's Greatest Sports Event" (the All-American Gravity Grand Prix) was begun in Akron, Ohio, in 1933.

**SOAP BOX DERBY #26 RACE CAR**   WYANDOTTE   LITHO TIN   1937
**SOAP BOX DERBY STEEL HELMET**   1930s

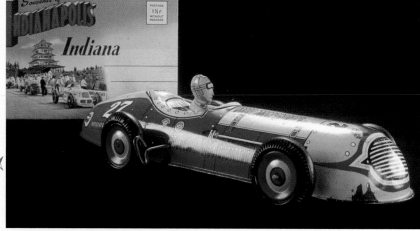

The first race at the Indianapolis 500-Mile Motor speedway took place in 1911 and was won by Ray Haroun in 6 hours and 42 minutes at an average speed of 74.6 miles-per hour.

**RACER #27**   MARX   TIN LITHO   MECHANICAL   12" LONG   1950

"Beautifully lithographed in many colors on heavy-gauge steel, and finished with durable, waterproof lacquer. These games are sanitary; can be washed when necessary. They are indestructible and will outlast any cardboard game."

**MOTOR RACE GAME W/4 CARS**   WOLVERINE   LITHO TIN   16-1/2" SQUARE   1926   89¢

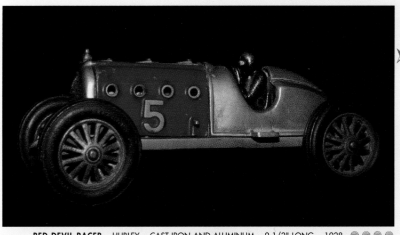

RED DEVIL RACER   HUBLEY   CAST IRON AND ALUMINUM   9-1/2" LONG   1928

➤ "Raise the hood and see
the motor."

"GOLDEN ARROW" RACER   HUBLEY   CAST IRON   6-3/4" LONG   1929

The low-to-the-ground real-life Golden Arrow ◁
racer was specially designed to race against time
and compete for a world speed record.

1953: Structure of DNA decoded;
Hillary and Norgay climb Mt. Everest.

RACE CAR   BUFFALO TOYS   LITHO TIN   MECHANICAL   19" LONG

➤ A spring pulled from the rear activates the
wheels of this striking, full-toned racer.

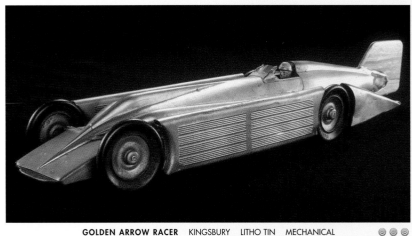

"Here it comes!...flashing down the track! With a roar it passes, setting a new speed record! Beautiful golden finish metal racer, built just like the powerful record breaker. Golden disc wheels with rubber tires. Front wheels turn like a real auto. Driver sits behind a transparent windshield. Rubber front bumpers protects furniture."

**GOLDEN ARROW RACER**    KINGSBURY    LITHO TIN    MECHANICAL
20" LONG    1929    (1935 PRICE: 89¢)

"On whirling disc winning auto makes rumbling noise like real racers at the speedway."

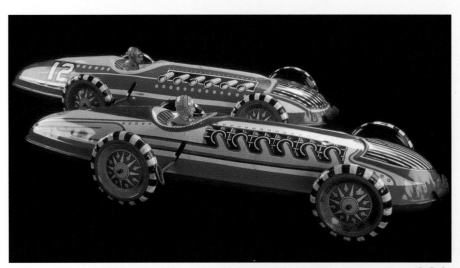

**RACE CARS**    MARX    LITHO TIN    MECHANICAL    16" LONG    1947

**AUTO RACE**    LITHO TIN    1931    $1

▷ "With huge soft rubber tires, car always lands right side up."

BOUNCING BENNY   MARX   LITHO TIN AND RUBBER   1939   45¢   ◎ ◎ ◎

▷ "After motor is wound, you can never tell just which car will win until the very end, because the cars keep swinging around—each in its own uncertainly moving track."

WEE WHIZ AUTO RACERS   MARX   MECHANICAL   11-1/4" DIAMETER   1927   ◎ ◎ ◎ ◎

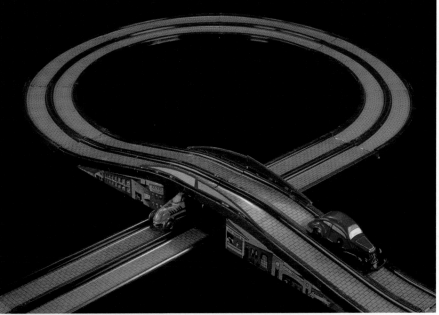

"A real speedway in the form of a figure 8 with Bridge ◁ Crossover. Consists of 16 interlocking sections and two streamline spring-wound cars. Cars race under and over the Bridge, around curves, and along straightaways."

CROSSOVER SPEEDWAY   MARX   LITHO TIN   144" DUAL TRACK   MECHANICAL CARS   1938   $1.89   ◎ ◎ ◎

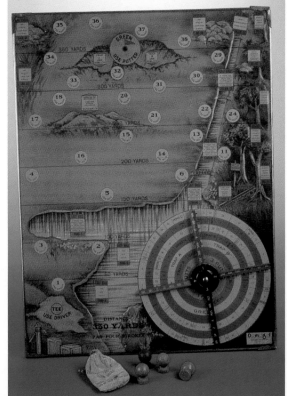

DOM-O-GOLF    DOMOGAME CO., INC.    LITHO TIN    1920s ◎ ◎

> Complicated or not, who could resist playing a game of Dom-O-Golf whose graphics were so sublime as this?

GOTHAM TOY DRIVING RANGE
GOTHAM PRESSED STEEL CORP.    LITHO TIN    1930s  ◎ ◎

> It was a kind of craze. People of all ages found that playing miniature golf helped keep their spirits up during the early years of the Depression. Four million Americans in 1934 putted balls through little windmills and mountains and Taj Mahals.

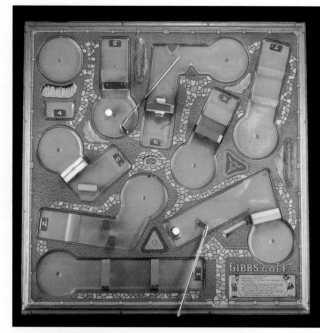

GIBBS GOLF    GIBBS MFG. CO.    LITHO TIN    LATE 1920s  ◎ ◎
(THE CLUBS PICTURED HERE ARE NOT ORIGINAL)

After striking the ball (assuming it's not dubbed)
the player is assured of getting his ball returned
to try again (it's called a Mulligan).

PLAY GOLF   STRAUSS   LITHO TIN   MECHANICAL   1929

Art Deco graphics make this one of the most sought-after bagatelles.

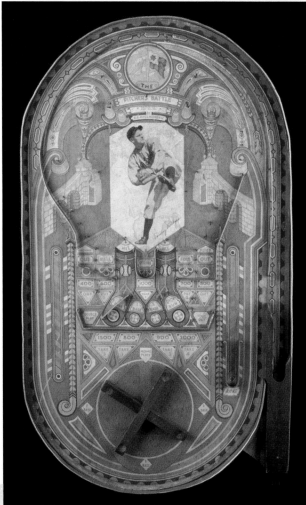

**THE PITCHER'S BATTLE**
R.G. KOLLMORGEN   LITHO PAPER ON WOOD   1935

**BAMBINO**   JOHNSON STOVE ELECTRIC CO.
LITHO TIN, RUBBER AND WOOD   1939

"Bambino is the only indoor baseball game using a real ball and bat. When ball is hit by player, the play, whether a strike, hit, or out is registered on the baseball board..."

Baseball was truly the national pastime of America.

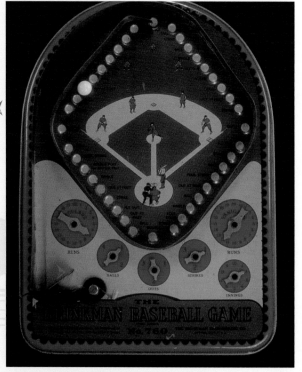

**BRINKMAN BASEBALL GAME**
BRINKMAN ENGINEERING CO.   LITHO TIN   1930s

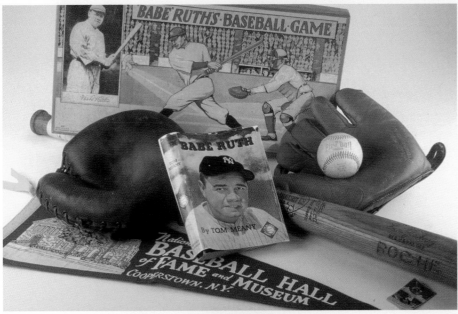

**BASEBALL GLOVES**
**BABE RUTH**   GROSSET AND DUNLAP
**BABE RUTH'S BASEBALL GAME**   MILTON BRADLEY   1930s   ◎ ◎ ◎ ◎
**PENNANT**

An unusual ◁
bagatelle: shoot the
marble in the slot
which then drops
onto a revolving
diamond for —
a single? an out?
a home run!

**PINCH HITTER BAGATELLE**   LITHO TIN   ◎ ◎ ◎
MECHANICAL   JOSEPH SCHNEIDER CO.   1937

**"SANDY ANDY" FULL BACK**   WOLVERINE   8" HIGH   1921   ◎ ◎ ◎

▷ When released the cocked foot of the
Sandy Andy Full Back kicks the football
far and sometimes straight.

**STAR BASKETBALL — INTERESTING GAME OF SKILL**
STAR PAPER BOX CO.   LATE 1920s

"Only the crack of the bat is missing to make your plays true to life. You direct your own play by pressing the lever at the top of game and after drum stops revolving, see what a strategist you've been. All combinations can be executed."

**THE GREAT AMERICAN GAME**   FRANTZ HARDWARE CO.
LITHO TIN   13-1/2" X 8-1/2"   1923   $1.65

"An adaptation of basketball played by 2 players with a Ping Pong ball. Above the court at either end hangs a basket into which each player tries to toss the ball by trigger action. So that the ball will always come to rest in the court above a trigger, and thus keep the game moving fast, the court has a series of depressions with a trigger at the bottom of each depression."

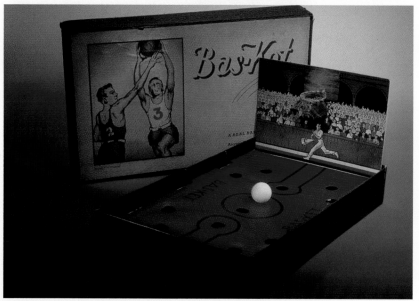

**BAS-KET BALL GAME**   CADACO LTD.   20" LONG   1947   $3.39

ALL STAR BASKET BALL GAME    WHITMAN PUBLISHING CO.    1936    19¢

"A rose can only smell
so achingly sweet to those

# america goes to war

who know that someday
they will die to its smell
and every joy and sorrow."

– WILLIAM SHAKESPEARE

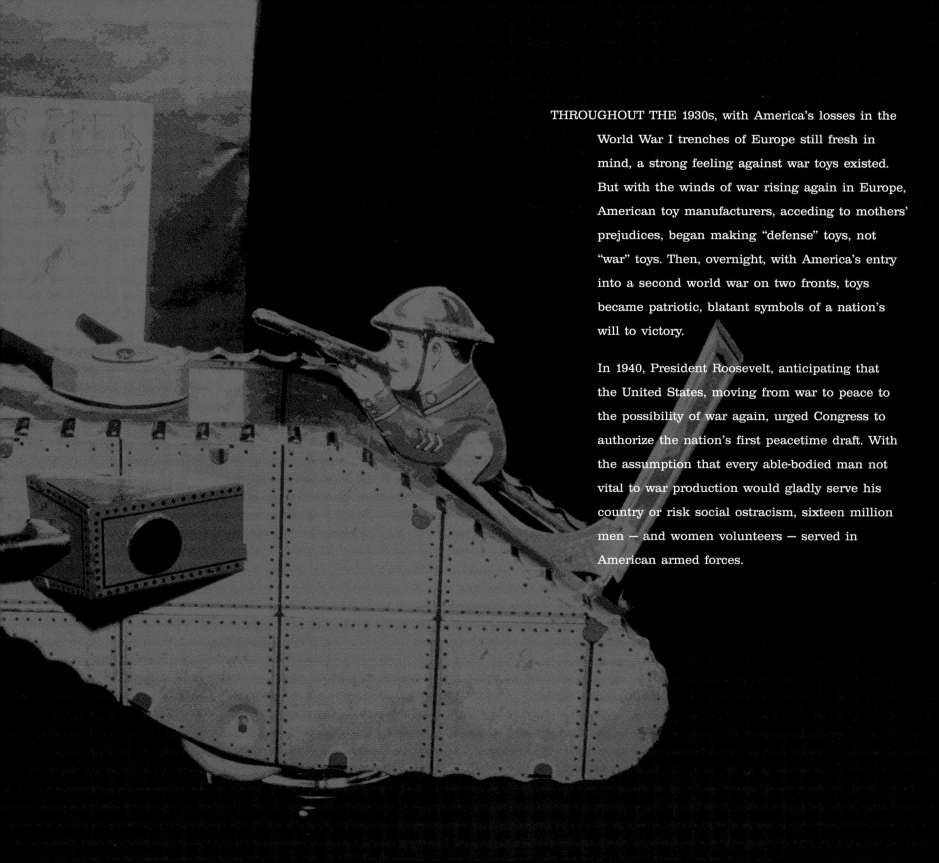

THROUGHOUT THE 1930s, with America's losses in the World War I trenches of Europe still fresh in mind, a strong feeling against war toys existed. But with the winds of war rising again in Europe, American toy manufacturers, acceding to mothers' prejudices, began making "defense" toys, not "war" toys. Then, overnight, with America's entry into a second world war on two fronts, toys became patriotic, blatant symbols of a nation's will to victory.

In 1940, President Roosevelt, anticipating that the United States, moving from war to peace to the possibility of war again, urged Congress to authorize the nation's first peacetime draft. With the assumption that every able-bodied man not vital to war production would gladly serve his country or risk social ostracism, sixteen million men — and women volunteers — served in American armed forces.

"Drummers actually play stirring march-rhythms. Each beat clearly accented. Action continuous."

FRONT ROW:
**LET THE DRUMMER BOY PLAY**  MARX  LITHO TIN  MECHANICAL  19" HIGH  1939  49¢
**BASS DRUMMER**  CHEIN  LITHO TIN  MECHANICAL  8-3/4" HIGH  1938  29¢
**BAND LEADER**  CHEIN  LITHO TIN  MECHANICAL  8-3/4" HIGH  1938  29¢
**BASS DRUMMER**  CHEIN  LITHO TIN  MECHANICAL  8-3/4" HIGH  1938  29¢
REAR: **15 CHEIN AND MARX SNARE DRUMMERS**  LITHO TIN  MECHANICAL

"An all-wood fort equipped with draw-bridge, winch, swivel shooting cannon, pennants, movable flag, fire step in court yard, moat gratings and electric entrance lamp connected to batteries and operated by switch in tower tops."

**KING ARTHUR'S FORT**   KEYSTONE   PRESSED WOOD   BATTERY LIGHT   20X17"   1935   89¢
**WOOD CANNON**   MANUFACTURER UNKNOWN   1920s
**BIG VICTORY (SPRING ACTION) CANNON**   LITHO TIN   MANUFACTURER UNKNOWN   1920s

**GEORGE THE DRUMMER BOY**
MARX   LITHO TIN   MECHANICAL   9" HIGH   1939   29¢

PLAY CASTLE AND BRIDGE  MARX  CARDBOARD  40" LONG  1932  33¢
CATERPILLAR TRACTOR  MARX

AFTER THE BATTLE THE REPORT HOME

"Realistically designed forts made of pressed cardboard which is stronger than wood and will not warp. Includes shooting cannons with dummy cannons and flags, also sliding doors. Finished in Bisque with brown stone and red towers."

THREE FORTS; SIEGE GUN W/STONE PARAPET  RICH TOYS  1936  (LARGE FORT $3.)  EACH: ⊚⊚

**LEAD SOLDIERS**   1930s TO 1940s   5-10¢ EACH
L. TO R: BARCLAY, BARCLAY, BARCLAY, MONOIL, MANOIL, MANOIL, BARCLAY, BARCLAY; JAYMAR TENT

**YOU'RE IN THE ARMY NOW BAGATELLE**
LITHO CARDBOARD AND TIN GOTHAM   c1942

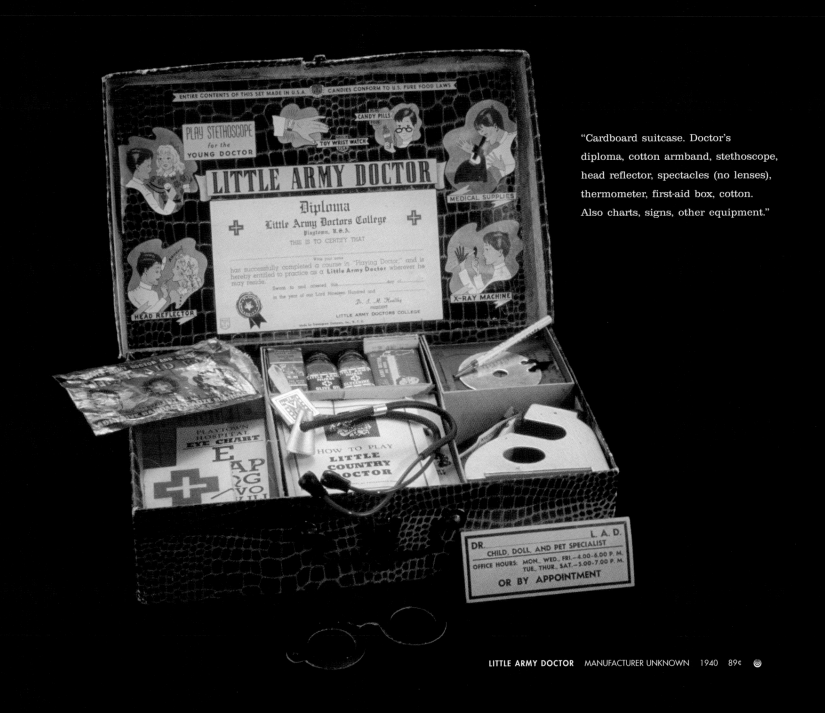

"Cardboard suitcase. Doctor's diploma, cotton armband, stethoscope, head reflector, spectacles (no lenses), thermometer, first-aid box, cotton. Also charts, signs, other equipment."

**LITTLE ARMY DOCTOR** MANUFACTURER UNKNOWN 1940 89¢

**VICTORY GLASS CRAFT SET**    AMERICAN TOY AND FURNITURE CO.    1944   ◉

**MOVIE VIEWS OF UNCLE SAM'S U. S. ARMY**    MANUFACTURER UNKNOWN    1940    65¢   ◉

**PERFECT PICTURE PUZZLE**    CONSOLIDATED TOY MANUFACTURING CO.    c1942   ◉

**AMERICA IN ACTION — THE PATRIOTIC ACTION PLAY BOOK**
MANUFACTURER UNKNOWN   1943

▷ A remarkable booklet that is a kind
of toy with cut-outs, fold-outs and a
little of everything pertaining to
America's winning the war.

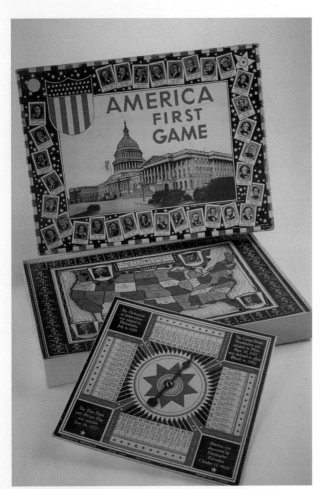

**AMERICA FIRST GAME**   DIAMOND TOY CO.   1939   25¢

**WARTIME AIRPLANE KITS**

GAMES OF WAR

"A handsome toy replica of a modern shooting gallery. The strong clockwork motor operates continuous belt to which various types of ships are attached, and pass in continuous action in front of target. Score is revealed when ships are shot down. Sturdy target pistol and 6 rubber suction cup darts included."

**ARMY AND NAVY TARGET**   MARX   LITHO TIN   ◎ ◎
MECHANICAL   17" LONG   1940   $2.75

"A jet of air keeps a ping-pong-like ball floating in front of and guarding the 1000 score as attempts are made to hit it away with a target pistol."

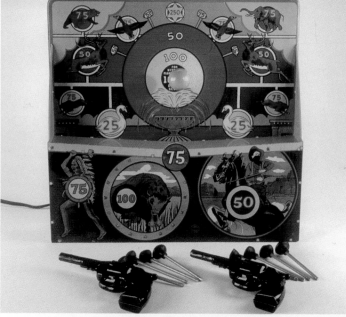

**ELECTRIC TARGET**   MARX   LITHO TIN   MECHANICAL/ELECTRIC   ◎ ◎
LATE 1940s-EARLY 1950s   $2.50

This patented gatling gun, handcranked, shoots out wood bullets.

**COAST DEFENSE GATTLING GUN W/WOODEN BULLETS**   BALDWIN MFG. CO.   1940

**SOLDIERS OF FORTUNE**  MARX  3-1/2"  2-DIMENSIONAL LITHO TIN SOLDIERS  c1940

› After Pearl Harbor, the United States went from a country using 1917 rifles to the strongest country the world had ever seen.

A whirling mechanism flings out 4 tiny airplanes w/ball bearing wheels. Where they land determines the score.

MAC 'MYSTERY GUN' W/FOUR TINY AIRPLANES ◎◎
MACDOWELL CO.    LITHO PRESSED STEEL    10"D    c1940

There are two openings in the colorful scene in which airplanes appear one at a time. The object is to shoot them down as fast as they appear with the 2 repeating elastic-firing 16" rifles.

WINGS TARGET GAME    PARKER BROS.    1940    $2    ◎◎

COAST DEFENSE TARGET GAME    WOLVERINE    LITHO TIN    EARLY 1940s    ◎◎

**AIR RAID DEFENSE BAGATELLE** ◉ ◉
GOTHAM PRESSED STEEL CO.   LITHO CARDBOARD AND TIN   1940s

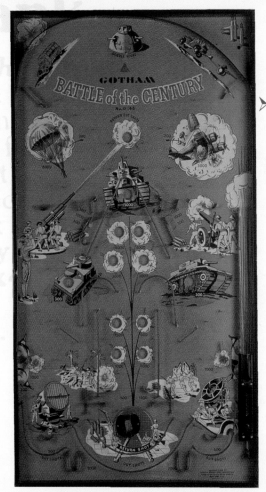

**BATTLE OF THE CENTURY BAGATELLE** ◉ ◉ ◉ ◉
GOTHAM   PRESSED STEEL CORP.
LITHO CARDBOARD AND TIN   BILL GRAHAM COLLECTION

> Superb graphics define this
> rare bagatelle game.

Another impressive wartime cardboard
standup target toy.

**AERO CHUTE ACTION TARGET** ◉ ◉
AMERICAN TOY WORKS CO.
LITHO CARDBOARD AND WOOD   EARLY 1940s

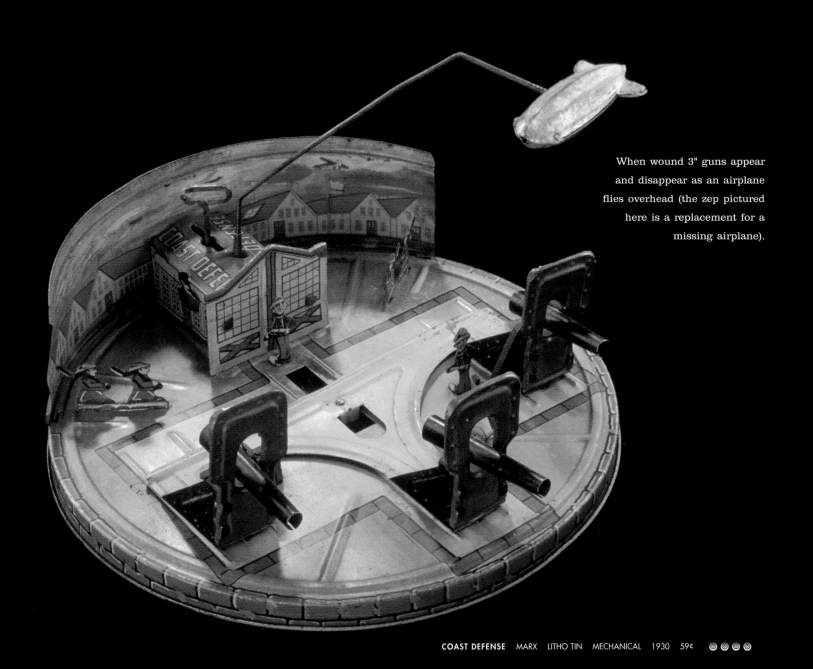

When wound 3" guns appear and disappear as an airplane flies overhead (the zep pictured here is a replacement for a missing airplane).

**COAST DEFENSE**  MARX  LITHO TIN  MECHANICAL  1930  59¢

"Boys! Be Ready For Enemy Air Attacks! You owe it to
your Uncle Sam to know what to do in the event of an
enemy air attack. The Junior Air Raid Warden kit has been
devised to enable you practice and play... You are furnished
with a Helmet, First Aid Kit, Bright Metal Badge, Report
sheets, Pencil and Note Book, Gas Mask and Splints...
Everyone of your friends will want to play with you...
you will become the most popular boy in the block."

**JUNIOR AIR RAID WARDEN KIT**   GILT EDGE TOY CO.   1942
$1.69 (PLUS POSTAGE)

A toy that commemorates soldiers returning from World War I,
marching to a band as an airplane circles overhead.

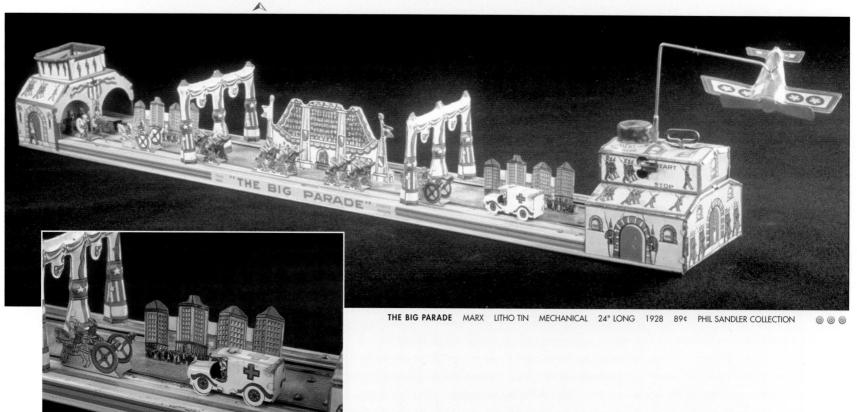

**THE BIG PARADE**   MARX   LITHO TIN   MECHANICAL   24" LONG   1928   89¢   PHIL SANDLER COLLECTION

"Wind the tank and it runs across the floor,
the doughboy pops out of the trapdoor,
aims, dodges back in again and trapdoor
shuts back in place. He repeats this action
many times as the tank zigzags along.
Four different actions."

In 1940 the United States
built 346 tanks.
In 1942, 24,000.

**DOUGHBOY TANK**   MARX   LITHO TIN   MECHANICAL   9-1/2" LONG   1930   89¢   ◎ ◎ ◎

"Just like the real army tanks with turret.
Made of heavy steel with solid rubber wheels.
Turret revolves by turning crank, noise maker
attached to crank gives machine-gun sound."

**WHIPPET TANK  STRUCTO**   PRESSED STEEL   MECHANICAL   12" LONG   1929   ◎ ◎ ◎
**"SUNNY ANDY" TANK**   WOLVERINE   PRESSED STEEL   MECHANICAL   14" LONG   1929   ◎ ◎ ◎
**TANK (W/BATTERY LIGHT)**   STRUCTO   PRESSED STEEL   12-1/2" LONG   1920   $1.25   ◎ ◎

**CANNON**   WOODHAVEN METAL STAMPING CO., INC.   LITHO TIN   23" OVERALL   EARLY 1930s

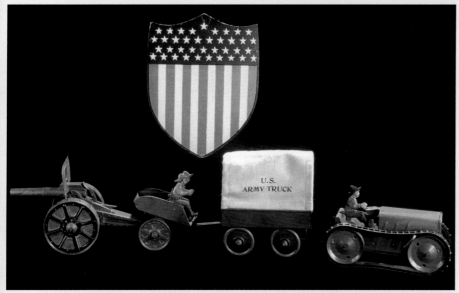

**U.S. ARMY SET: TRACTOR, TRUCK, CAISSON, CANNON**   MARX   LITHO TIN   MECHANICAL   1935   ◎◎◎◎

**CRAWLING SOLDIERS**   MARX   LITHO TIN   MECHANICAL   7-3/4" LONG   ◎◎

**U.S. ARMY TRAINING CENTER**   MARX   LITHO TIN   1950s

"Hope, unlike optimism, derives not from visions of the future but from memories of the past,

america enters a new age

memories in which the experience of order and contentment was so intense that subsequent disillusionments can not dislodge it."

– CHRISTOPHER LASCH

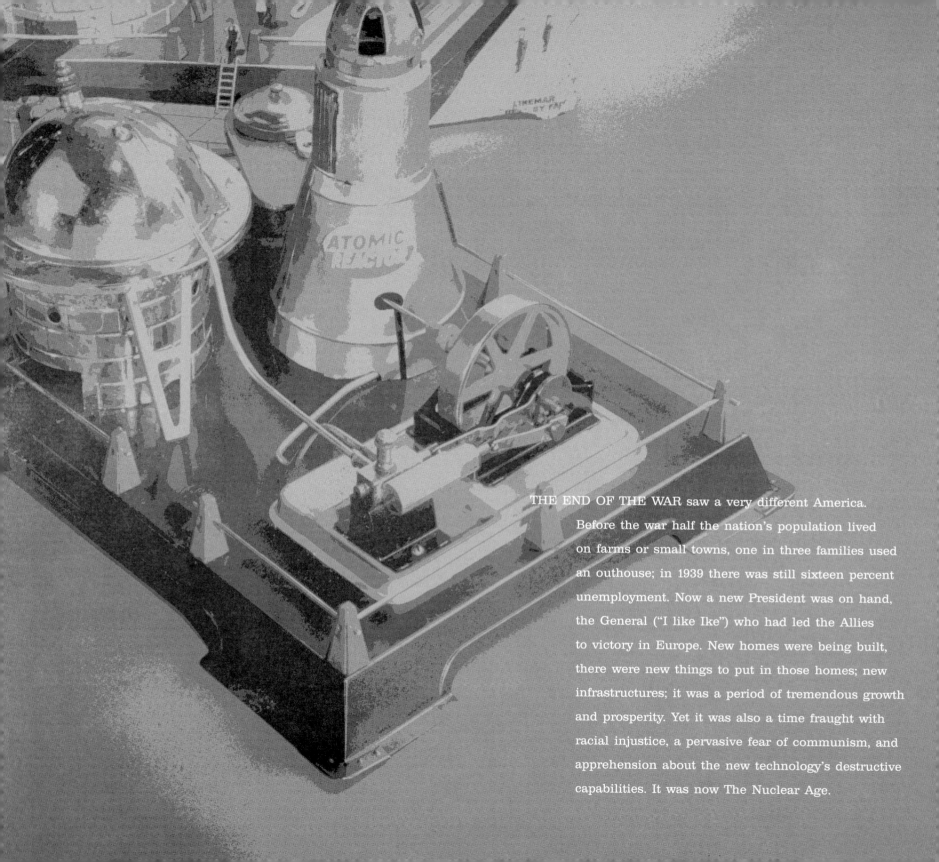

THE END OF THE WAR saw a very different America. Before the war half the nation's population lived on farms or small towns, one in three families used an outhouse; in 1939 there was still sixteen percent unemployment. Now a new President was on hand, the General ("I like Ike") who had led the Allies to victory in Europe. New homes were being built, there were new things to put in those homes; new infrastructures; it was a period of tremendous growth and prosperity. Yet it was also a time fraught with racial injustice, a pervasive fear of communism, and apprehension about the new technology's destructive capabilities. It was now The Nuclear Age.

DELIVER-ALL SCOOTER   NYLINT   1950

ICE CREAM SCOOTER   COURTLAND   LITHO TIN   MECHANICAL   1952
**CLIMBING MONKEY MARBLE TOY**
EMPORIUM SPECIALTY CO.   LITHO TIN   1950
**BOARDWALK SCOOTER**   WYANDOTTE   LITHO TIN   MECHANICAL   1954

MARSHALL FIELD TRUCK   TONKA   PRESSED STEEL   22" LONG   1954   ⦿ ⦿ ⦿ ⦿

**MODERN KITCHEN SET**   MARX   LITHO TIN   1950   ◎ ◎

**SKYSCRAPER GAME**   PARKER BROTHERS   1937   ◎

**CLIMBING FIREMEN**   MARX   LITHO TIN   MECHANICAL   ◎ ◎ ◎
23" HIGH LADDER   1935   47¢ (ONE FIREMAN TO A SET)

**JOHN CAMERON SWAYZE WORLD NEWS GAME**   MILTON BRADLEY CO.   1954

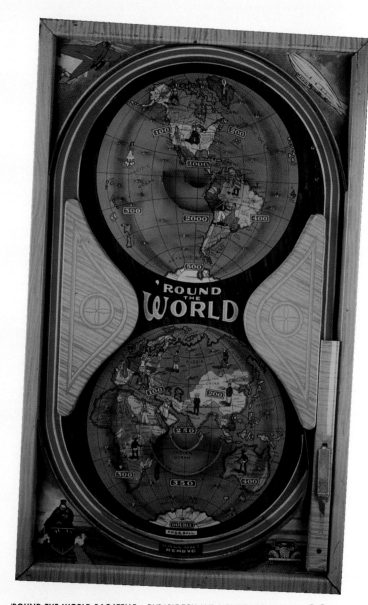

**'ROUND THE WORLD BAGATELLE**   DURABLE TOY AND NOVELTY CO.   1940

**SPACE SCIENTIST DRAFTING SET**　HASSENFELD BROS.　1951
**727-K ROBOT**　MARX　PLASTIC; BATTERY OPERATED　12" HIGH　1957　$5.98

**ATOMIC REACTOR STEAM ENGINE**　LINEMAR　LITHO TIN/ALUMINUM　1954

"Children know "Flash Gordon" — he's the popular hero in many newspaper cartoons and this is the Pistol he carries on his adventures everywhere."

"Futuristic signal gun used by Flash Gordon. Trigger activates a loud siren, nozzle emits harmless flint sparks."

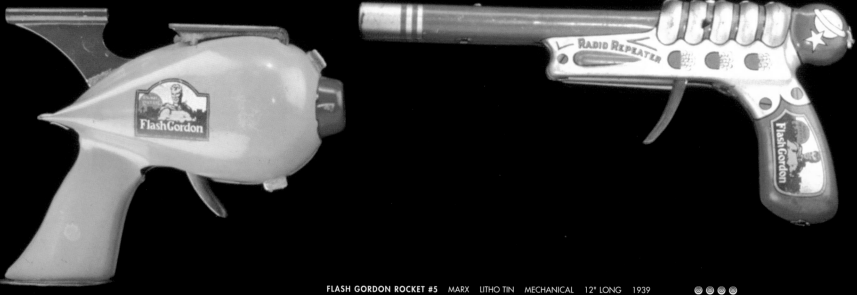

**FLASH GORDON ROCKET #5**   MARX   LITHO TIN   MECHANICAL   12" LONG   1939
**FLASH GORDON RADIO REPEATER PISTOL** (CLICK ACTION)   MARX   LITHO TIN   10" LONG   1935   10¢
**FLASH GORDON SIGNAL PISTOL**   MARX   LITHO TIN   7-3/4" LONG   1935   44¢

THE SPACE TOYS OF THE 1930s excited the minds of an entire generation of American youth and helped make potential scientific and technological exploits in outer space part of the national consciousness. Now there were real space ships and real robots. There was an eerie mystique about them but a dark side too — the nagging possibility that they might run amok like Dr. Frankenstein's monster. Had we, in our human quest for knowledge, and in an ever expanding world that had, at the same time, become smaller, and scarier, made a Faustian bargain?

# epilogue

Toys, to an archeologist, are like potsherds, reflecting a culture's aspirations, its energies and its values. Toys bespeak the culture that made them, that put them in the hands of its children. Or at least they used to. Whether they do so today remains to be seen.

For nearly two centuries American toys encouraged children to fantasize about joining the adult world. They encouraged a relationship to history, specifically American history. Today, instead of encouraging children to aspire to adulthood (as we elders define adulthood), toys represent an anarchic world independent of grownups, disconnected from political and social awareness and absent of historical memory.

Children today expect some sort of stimulation from their toys. The following would not be an unrepresentative sampling of

what you will find in the local Toy World/Toys R Us stores...

• Rambo First-Blood
• Masters of the Universe — The Evil Horde Fright
• Headmaster Skull Cruncher
• Gotcha Enforcer Set
• Phototon Electric Warrior Battle Gun
• Spurious Armored Battle Station
• Proton Blaster — Captain Power and the Soldiers of the Future
• Princess of Power Doll
• Go For It — The Game Where You Can Have It All

Like the "antique" toys presented in this book, contemporary toys are mass-produced, but mass-produced with a vengeance: molded of plastic and machine assembled with push-button electronics, they celebrate materialistic, aggressive, even death-dealing vices, not virtues. They have little resemblance to "reality."

Or do they?

*The more things change, the more they remain the same.*

Childhood in America today is very different from childhoods of the past and it can be no surprise that today's childrens' toys (like their clothes, music, mores, study, and recreational activities) are also very different: there is no limit to what they may imagine in fact. Literally anything is possible for them to do materially, or, we are told, soon will be possible. Nor can we be further surprised that their energies are little attuned to the past but to the possibilities, even the probabilities, of their attaining (happily or unhappily) whatever unknowable place the world is headed towards.

For the most part charmless, many of today's toys are, however, admittedly fascinating. The way, for instance, they can be transformed from one thing to another — a robot into a rocket into a (whatever) — as its young owner figures out problems in commuting from earth to Mars to Venus to...

(It's too exhausting to think about).

Flash Gordon, Buck Rogers and Wilma —

they were the astronauts that we parents and grandparents knew. They were cartoon characters. They weren't real. Today's toys are imaginary too, but they are not, I think, without "reality" — a different kind of reality, one that is amorphous, uninstitutionalized,
tentative as well as aggressive (there is very little humor in today's toys), a psychic reflection of the world more than a literal one.

No one, least of all myself, can know the good or bad effects of today's inorganic "fantasy" toys on children's attitudes to life, toys that do not have pasts and futures to hope for but seem only to have a self-satisfied, superficial and essentially hedonistic, ugly present. What is difficult to imagine is that there will be many children, fifty years from now who will look at their toys of childhood with the same merited admiration that we parents and grandparents hold for the toys portrayed in this book. With barely muted alarm we try not to think that such toys may in fact suggest our progeny's futures. It will not, however, be for us to know. What we do know is that toys not only reflect their era but have from the late nineteenth century on become harbingers of the ever new world of tomorrow. We'll cross our fingers.

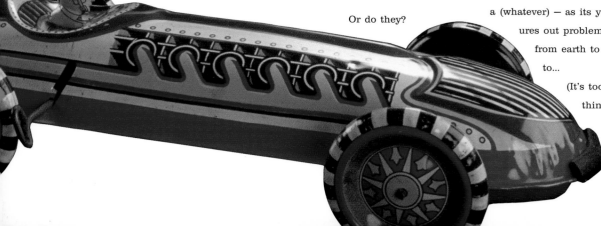

# u.s. patent dates

# money conversion

Dating a toy can be generally known in those instances in which patent numbers are given to a toy or its box. Not all toys, it should be noted, were sold the same year as their patent date.

To convert a toy's original retail price to 2000 dollars —

| YEAR | PATENT NUMBER | YEAR | PATENT NUMBER |
|------|---------------|------|---------------|
| 1920 | 1,326,899 | 1938 | 2,101,004 |
| 1921 | 1,364,063 | 1939 | 2,142,080 |
| 1922 | 1,401,948 | 1940 | 2,185,170 |
| 1923 | 1,440,362 | 1941 | 2,227,418 |
| 1924 | 1,478,996 | 1942 | 2,268,540 |
| 1925 | 1,521,590 | 1943 | 2,307,007 |
| 1926 | 1,568,040 | 1944 | 2,338,081 |
| 1927 | 1,612,790 | 1945 | 2,366,154 |
| 1928 | 1,654,521 | 1946 | 2,391,856 |
| 1929 | 1,696,897 | 1947 | 2,413,675 |
| 1930 | 1,742,181 | 1948 | 2,433,824 |
| 1931 | 1,787,424 | 1949 | 2,457,797 |
| 1932 | 1,839,190 | 1950 | 2,492,944 |
| 1933 | 1,892,663 | 1951 | 2,536,016 |
| 1934 | 1,944,449 | 1952 | 2,580,379 |
| 1935 | 1,985,878 | 1953 | 2,624,046 |
| 1936 | 2,026,510 | 1954 | 2,664,562 |
| 1937 | 2,066,309 | 1955 | 2,698,434 |

| YEAR | MULTIPLY |
|------|----------|
| 1920 | 8.60 |
| 1925 | 9.83 |
| 1930 | 10.30 |
| 1934 | 12.84 |
| 1940 | 12.29 |
| 1946 | 8.82 |
| 1950 | 7.14 |
| 1955 | 6.42 |

# american toy manufacturers

**All-Fair** (Alderman-Fairchild Co.)
Churchville, NY 1922-1950s
Harry Alderman and Elmer
Fairchild, founders

**Allied Manufacturing Co.**
Chicago, IL

**American Art Clay Co.**
Indianapolis, IN

**American Crayon Co.**
Sandusky, OH

**American Flyer**
Chicago, IL

**American Game & Toy Co.**
Brooklyn, NY

**American Lead Pencil Co.**

**American Toy & Furniture Co.**
Chicago, IL

**American Toy Works**

**American Toys**

**Animate Toy Co.**
New York, NY

**Arcade Manufacturing Co.**
Freeport, IL 1893-1942

**Auburn Rubber Co.**
Auburn, IN 1935-1969

**Automatic Toy Co.**
Staten Island, NY

**Baldwin Manufacturing Co.**
Brooklyn, NY

**B & R Company**

**The Bambino Products Co.**
Chicago, IL 1934

**Barclay Manufacturing Co.**
W. Hoboken, NY 1924-1971
Leon Druze and Michael Levy,
founders

**George Borgfeldt Co.**
New York, NY 1881-1962
Distributors of no-name toys

**Boycraft & Co.**
New York, NY
1881-1962

**Bradford Co.**
New York, NY

**Milton Bradley Co.**
Springfield, MA
1860-present

**Brinkman Engineering Co.**
Dayton, OH

**Buddy L**
(Moline Pressed Steel Co.)
Moline, IL 1910-1936
Fred Lundahl, founder

**Fritz Bueschel**
Hacketstown, NJ

**Buffalo Toy & Tool Works**
Buffalo, NY 1924-1968

**Built-Rite**
Lafayette, IN 1935-1956

**Cadaco Ltd.**
Leandro, CA

**Cameo Doll Co.**

**Canterbury Sales Co.**
Chicago, IL

**N. D. Cass Co.**
Athol, MA 1894-?

**Castle Cine Art**

**J. Chein & Co.**
Harrison, NY 1903-1948

**J. Chein Industries**
Burlington, NJ 1948-present

**Chicago Roller Skate Co.**
Chicago, IL

**T. J. Cleghorn Co.**
Lowell, MA

**Cleveland Model Airplane Co.**
Cleveland, OH

**Comet Model Airplane Co.**
Chicago, IL

**Conestoga Corporation**
Bethlehem, PA

**Control Mfg. Co.**
Camden, NJ 1944-1951

**Cor-cor** (Corcoran Mfg. Co.)
Washington, IN 1920s-1940s
Louis A. Corcoran, founder

**Courtland Mfg. Co.**
Camden, NJ; Philadelphia, PA
1944-1971

**Cracker Jack Co.**
Chicago, IL

**Crown Toy Co.**

**Daisy Corporation**
(Iron Windmill Co.)
Plymouth, MI 1882-1958;
Rogers, AR 1958-present

**Dayton Friction Toy Works**
Dayton, OH 1909-1935
D. P. Clark, founder

**Nelson Delavan Co.**
Seneca Falls, NY 1950-1953

**Dell Publishing Co.**

**Dent Hardware Co.**
Fullerton, PA 1895-1975
Henry H. Dent and three partners,
founders

**Devry Corporation**
Chicago, IL

**Diamond Toy Co.**
Wilmington, DE

**Dolly Toy Co.**
Dayton, OH

**Domogame Co., Inc.**
New York, NY

**Durable Toy & Novelty Co.**
New York, NY

**Dyna Model Products Co.**
Oyster Bay, Long Island, NY
1930s-1940s

**Eagle Pencil Co.**
New York, NY 1934

**Effenbee Doll Co.**
New York, NY

**Einsen-Freeman Co., Inc.**
Long Island City, NY

**Emporium Specialty Co.**

**Ertl**
Dyersburg, IA 1945-present

**Excel**

**Fisher-Price, Ltd.**
E. Aurora, NY 1930-present
Herman Fisher and Irving Price,
founders

**Fulton Specialty Co.**
Elizabeth, NJ

**Gibbs Manufacturing Co.**
Canton, OH 1884-present
Lewis E. Gibbs, founder

**Gilt Edge Toy Co.**

**Girard Manufacturing Co.**
Girard, PA 1920s-1930s

**Grey Iron** (Greycraft)
Mt. Joy, PA 1903-?
Edward Musser and Samuel
Schmidt, founders

**Halsom Block Co.**
Chicago, IL 1919-1962
Hal Eliot and Sam Goss, founders

**Harding Products**

**Hassenfeld Bros.**
Central Falls, RI

**N. N. Hill Brass Co.**
E. Hampton, CT 1889-1960s

**Hoge Manufacturing Co.**
(A Henry Katz organization)
Hoge toys reportedly manufactured
by Girard. Active in 1920s.

**Home Foundry Co.**
Chicago, IL

**Hubley Manufacturing Co.**
Lancaster, PA 1894-present
John E. Hubley, founder. Ceased
cast iron toy production by 1940.

**Hulles Toys**

**Hustler Toy Corporation**
(Frantz Hardware; Frantz Mfg. Co.)
Sterling, IL

**Interplay Goods Co.**

**Jaymar**

**Jeanette Toy & Novelty Co.**
Jeanette, PA 1898-present

**Paul Jones Model Airplane Co.**

**Kenton Hardware Co.**
Kenton, OH 1890-1952

**Kep & Lane, Inc.**
Leroy, NY

**Keystone Film Co.**

**Keystone Manufacturing Co.**
Boston, MA 1922-?
Chester Rimmer and Arthur
Jackson, founders.
Originally named Jacrim.

**Kilgore Manufacturing Co.**
Westerville, OH Produced toys
1920-1940s; closed 1978.

**Kingsbury Manufacturing Co.**
Keene, NH 1919-1942
Harry Thayer, founder

**Knapp Electric and Novelty Co.**
Port Chester, NY; Indianapolis, IN

**Knickerbocker Co.**
N. Hollywood, CA

**Knickerbocker Doll Co.**
New York, NY

R. G. Kollmorgen

**Lavelle Co.**
New Haven, CT

**Liberty Playthings**
Niagara Falls, NY
late 1920s-early 1930s

**Lindstrom Tool and Toy Co.**
Bridgeport, CT   1813-1940s

**Linemar**
Marx's Japanese subsidiary

**Lionel Corporation**
New York, NY

**Live Long Toy Co.**
Chicago, IL

**Manoil**
Waverly, NY   1934-1955
Jack Manoil, founder

**Mark Co.**
Chicago, IL

**Marks Bros.**
Boston, MA

**Louis Marx & Co.**
New York, NY 1919-1979
Louis Marx, founder

**McDowell Manufacturing Co.**
Pittsburgh, PA

**Marelco**
Portland, OR

**Mechanical Metal Stamping Corp.**
Brooklyn, NY

**Megow Model Airplane Shop**
Philadelphia, PA

**Mengel Playthings**
St. Louis, MO

**Metalcraft**
St. Louis, MO

**Miners, Inc.**
New York, NY

**National Game Co.**
Portland, OR

**Naylor Corporation**
Chicago, IL

**New York Toy & Novelty Co.**
New York, NY

**Neubert & Rode Toy Co.**
Jeanette, PA

**Newton & Thomas Mfg. Co.**
Drayden, UT

**Nifty** (Distributed by George
Borgfeldt Co.) Philadelphia, PA

**Northwestern Products Co.**
St. Louis, MO

**Novel Products Co.**
Chicago, IL

**Nylint Tool & Mfg. Co.**
Rockford, IL   1937-present
(toy production began in 1946)
David Nyberg and David Klint,
founders

**Ohio Art**
Bryan, OH   1908-present Began
producing toys in 1917.
H. S. Winzeler, founder

**Orkin**
Cambridge, MA
Samuel Orkin, founder

**Orkin Craft**
(Calwis Industries, Ltd.)
Beverly Hills, CA   1935-1936

**Joe Ott Model Airplane Co.**

**Parker Brothers**
Salem, MA

**M. Pochapin, Inc.**
New York, NY

**Porter Chemical Co.**
Hagerstown, NY

**J. Pressman & Co.**

**Quadriga Toy Co.**

**Quester Corporation**
New York, NY   1952-present

**Ranger Steel Products**
Roslyn Heights, NY

**Rappaport Bros., Inc.**
Roslyn heights, NY

**Reeves Manufacturing Co.**
Milford, CT   1888-?

**Rempel Manufacturing Co.**
Akron, OH

**Republic Tool Products Co.**
Dayton, OH   1922-1932
Charles F. Black and Elijah Miller,
founders

**Rich Manufacturing Co.**
Sterling; Morris, IL; Clinton, IA
Maurice and Edward Rich,
founders

**Rittenhouse**

**Rosebud Art Co.**
New York, NY

**Saalfield Publishing Co.**
Akron, OH

**Schieble**
Dayton, OH   1909-1931
William E. Schieble, founder

**Joseph Schneider, Inc.**

**Schoenhut**
1872-1935

**Scott Manufacturing Co.**
Chicago, IL

**Selchow & Righter**
New York, NY

**Selrite**

**Smith-Miller** (Smitty Toys)
Santa Monica, CA   1945-1955

**Son-ny Toys**

**South Bend Toy Mfg. Co., Inc.**
South Bend, IN

**Spear Co.**

**Standard Solophone Mfg. Co.**
New York, NY

**Statler Manufacturing Co., Inc.**
Baltimore, MD

**Ferdinand Strauss Corporation**
New York, NY   early 1900s-1944
Ferdinand Strauss, founder
Manufactured toys 1914-1927.

**Strombeck-Becker Mfg. Co.**
Moline, IL   1929-1961

**Structo Manufacturing Co.**
Freeport, IL   1908-1975
Louis and Edward Strohacker,
C. C. Thompson, founders

**Sturditoys**
(The Sturditoy Corporation)
Providence, RI   1929-1933
Victor C. Wetzel, president

# bibliography

Aune, Al
*Arcade Toys*
Robert F. Mannella

Bettelheim, Bruno
*The Uses of Enchantment*
Random House

Glassner, Lester
*Dime Store Days*
Penquin Books

Gottschaulk, Lillian
*American Toy Cars and Trucks*
Abbeville Press

Harmon, Kenny
*Comic Strip Toys*
Wallace-Homestead Book Co.

Heide, Robert/Gilman, John
*Cartoon Collectibles*
Double Day

Heide, Robert/Gilman, John
*Dime Store Dream Parade*
E. P. Dutton

Hewitt, Karen
Roomet, Louise
*Educational Toys in America —
1800 to the Present*
Robert Hull Fleming Museum

Hillier, Bevis
*Mickey Mouse Memorabilia*
Harry N. Abrams, Inc.

Horsham, Michael
*'20s & '30s Style*
Chartwell Books, Inc.

Lesser, Robert
*A Celebration of Art and Memorabilia*
Hawthorn Books

Long, Earnest and Ida
*Dictionary of Toys Sold in America,
Volumes I and 2*   (self-pub.)

Mathews, Jack
*Toys Go To War*
Pictorial Histories Publications Co.

McCullough, Albert
*New Book of Buddy "L" Toys,
Volumes 1 and 2*
Greenberg Pub.

Jaffe, Allen
*J.Chein & Co. A Collectors Guide
to an American Toy Maker*
Schiffer Books

Milet, Jaques/Forbes, Robert
*Toy Boats*
Charles Scribners Sons

Mumsey, Cecil
*Disneyana: Walt Disney Collectibles*
Hawthorn Books

Muensterberger, Werner
*Collecting: An Unruly Passion*
Harcourt

O'Brien, Richard
*Collecting Toys*
Krause Publications

O'Brien, Richard
*The Story of American Toys*
Abbeville Press

Strange, Craig
*Tinker Toys*
Collector Books

Whitehill, Bruce
*Games*
Wallace-Homestead Book Co.

**CATALOGS:**
Montgomery Ward; Sears Roebuck;
Spiegel

**PERIODICALS:**
*Antique Toy World; Collector's Showcase;
The Inside Collector*

# about the photographers　　about the author

Larry Evans (Larry Evans Photography, Chicago) is a Chicago commercial photographer with major national and international clients. Before opening his own studio, he was for seventeen years Photography Director for *Outside* magazine. He holds a Bachelor of Arts degree from Brooks Institute of Photography.

Charles Sharp began his career as a CBS television newsman, then formed and directed his own documentary film company, Cameras International, for eleven years and for fifteen years was associate professor of filmmaking at the Institute of Design, Illinois Institute of Technology. He is author of a novel, *The Great River* and a non-fiction work, *An All-American Girl*.

Robert Frerck, a former student of Charles Sharp at IIT's Institute of Design, is founder/owner of Odyssey Productions, a supplier of geographic photography to the world's media. Frerck's award-winning photographs regularly appear in *National Geographic*, *Time*, et al. He is the author/photographer of two books, *Eternal Spain*, and *Eternal Mexico*.

Charles Dee Sharp was teaching full-time as associate professor of Cinema Studies at the Institute of Design, Illinois Institute of Technology, when he began to feel a persistent fatigue, along with memory loss, rubbery legs, and a vague numbness in his right arm. His symptoms growing ever more acute, he saw numerous Chicago doctors and three times visited the Mayo Clinic. Unable to drive with his wife and daughter to their weekend Indiana farm, he was forced to sell the farm, his car, and retire from teaching. Finally diagnosed at the University of Illinois as having multiple sclerosis, he was given massive cortisone treatments one year apart to no lasting effect. Learning of a British lawyer/screenwriter who had devised a plan which he theorized might alleviate his own MS symptoms and which over time might allow him to walk (Roger McDougal was originally in a wheelchair unable to button his shirt), Sharp, all medical and non-medical modalities having failed, began following McDougal's diet rigorously (the essentials: no refined sugar, animal fat or gluten). Coincidentally, one of Sharp's former graduate students tele-phoned him that he thought he'd seen a toy train in a collectibles shop such as the one Sharp had off-handedly spoken about one day in class, a toy professor Sharp said he'd had as a boy. The former student took Sharp to the shop and Sharp bought the train. Too fatigued to read a newspaper, Sharp played with the train, like a child, for hours. Learning of a national toy show taking place in a Chicago suburb, he asked to be driven to it. The aisles of old toys amazed him, inspirited him. In the following months he forced himself onto his bicycle to scout out antique shops where he might occasionally discover toys he'd had as a child — or wished he'd had. Thus it went through the years. There were long periods when he was virtually immobilized by fatigue but imperceptibly — with the combination of Roger McDougal's diet and the JOY of finding and collecting the toys of his childhood — Sharp, his MS increasingly in remission with only occasional flareups, today enjoys the energy and steadfastness of most anyone his age.

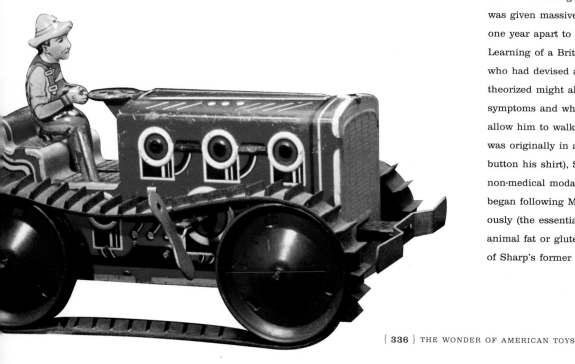